Deconstruction and Pragmatism

Is pragmatism deconstructive? Is deconstruction pragmatic? These questions are levelled at two of the most prominent thinkers of our time. Richard Rorty and Jacques Derrida are brought together in this collection in dialogue to discuss their respective positions.

Both Derrida and Rorty have been the focus of controversy not least because the implications of their work radically undermine the dominant rationalist approach. Whilst their perspectives are very different, their common rejection of a foundationalist conception of philosophy locates them on the same side in a number of debates, particularly those concerning the legacy of the Enlightenment.

This book is the record of a symposium to discuss, amongst other things, how Derrida's deconstruction and Rorty's pragmatism could contribute to a nonfoundationalist theory of democracy. Apart from Derrida and Rorty, two other eminent theorists took part in the discussion, Simon Critchley and Ernesto Laclau. They brought forward the points of convergence as well as the differences in both approaches and examined their political relevance.

Anyone interested in current theoretical and political debates, and the work of Jacques Derrida and Richard Rorty, should read *Deconstruction and Pragmatism*.

'In recent years there have been some striking convergences between Pragmatism and Deconstruction. But there are also significant ways in which these philosophical orientations swerve away from each other and seem incommensurable. Chantal Mouffe's lucid introduction sets the stage for a lively exchange between Richard Rorty and Jacques Derrida. Their crossfire is enriched by the contributions of Simon Critchley and Ernesto Laclau. Altogether a splended and illuminating feast of agonistic debate'

Richard J. Bernstein,
Vera List Professor of Philosophy,
Graduate Faculty, New School for Social Research

Chantal Mouffe is a Senior Research Fellow at the Centre for the Study of Democracy at the University of Westminster.

Deconstruction and Pragmatism

Simon Critchley, Jacques Derrida,
Ernesto Laclau and
Richard Rorty

Edited by Chantal Mouffe

London and New York

First published 1996
by Routledge
11 New Fetter Lane, London EC4P 4EE

Simultaneously published in the USA and Canada
by Routledge
29 West 35th Street, New York, NY 10001

Routledge is an International Thomson Publishing company

© 1996 Selection of editorial matter: 1996 Chantal Mouffe;
individual chapters to individual authors

Typeset in Palatino by
Ponting–Green Publishing Services, Chesham, Bucks

Printed and bound in Great Britain by
Clays Ltd, St Ives, PLC

British Library Cataloguing in Publication Data
A catalogue record for this book is available from the British Library

Library of Congress Cataloguing in Publication Data
Deconstruction and pragmatism / Simon Critchley . . . [et al.] ; edited
  by Chantal Mouffe.
        p.   cm.
  Includes bibliographical references and index.
  1. Derrida, Jacques. 2. Rorty, Richard. 3. Deconstruction.
  4. Pragmatism.   I. Critchley, Simon, 1960– . II. Mouffe,
  Chantal.
  B2430.D484D39   1996
  149dc20

                                                    95–26619
                                                    CIP

ISBN 0–415–12169–8 (hbk)
ISBN 0–415–12170–1 (pbk)

Contents

Notes on Contributors

Simon Critchley is Reader in Philosophy at the University of Essex. He is the author of *The Ethics of Deconstruction, Very Little ... Almost Nothing* and co-editor of *Re-Reading Levinas, Deconstructive Subjectivities, Blackwell's Companion to Continental Philosophy* and *Emmanuel Levinas: Basic Philosophical Writings*.

Jacques Derrida is Directeur d'Études at the École des Hautes Études en Sciences Sociales in Paris. His principal texts include *Speech and Phenomena, Writing and Difference, Of Grammatology, Dissemination, Margins of Philosophy, The Post Card, Given Time, Limited Inc, Specters of Marx* and *The Politics of Friendship*.

Ernesto Laclau is Professor of Politics at the University of Essex. He is the author of *New Reflections on the Revolutions of Our Time* and *Emancipation(s)*, co-author of *Hegemony and Socialist Strategy* and editor and contributor to *The Making of Political Identities*.

Chantal Mouffe is the Quintin Hogg Senior Research Fellow at the Centre for the Study of Democracy at the University of Westminster and a member of the Collège International de Philosophie in Paris. She is the author of, among other works, *The Return of the Political* and *Hegemony and Socialist Strategy* (with Ernesto Laclau), and the editor of *Dimensions of Radical Democracy*.

Richard Rorty is University Professor of Humanities at the University of Virginia. He is the author of many books including *Philosophy and the Mirror of Nature, Consequences of Pragmatism, Essays on Heidegger and Others, Objectivity, Relativism and Truth*, and *Contingency, Irony and Solidarity*.

Acknowledgements

This volume has its origin in a symposium on 'Deconstruction and Pragmatism' that I organized at the Collège International de Philosophie in Paris on May 29, 1993.

I am very grateful to Noreen Harburt for the time she spent in transcribing the tapes and to Simon Critchley for translating Derrida's remarks into English.

Chantal Mouffe

1

Deconstruction, Pragmatism and the Politics of Democracy

Chantal Mouffe

Jacques Derrida and Richard Rorty are at the centre of many controversies and this is not surprising since the implication of their work is radically to undermine the very basis of the dominant rationalist approach. It is no wonder then that Derrida's deconstruction and Rorty's new pragmatism have been repeatedly decried by traditional philosophers. This has not prevented their books, however, from exerting a major influence; indeed, their impact has been felt world-wide. Their perspectives are, no doubt, very different but their common rejection of a foundationalist conception of philosophy locates them on the same side in a great number of debates, especially those concerning the legacy of the Enlightenment.

Derrida and Rorty are at one in refusing Habermas's claim that there exists a necessary link between universalism, rationalism and modern democracy and that constitutional democracy represents a moment in the unfolding of reason, linked to the emergence of universalist forms of law and morality. They both deny the availability of an Archimedean point – such as Reason – that could guarantee the possibility of a mode of argumentation that would have transcended its particular conditions of enunciation.

Nevertheless, their critique of rationalism and universalism does not prevent them being strongly committed to the defence of the political side of the Enlightenment, the democratic project. Their disagreement with Habermas is not political but theoretical. They share his engagement with democratic politics but they consider that democracy does not need philosophical foundations and that it is not through rational grounding that its institutions could be made secure.

To stress the existence of a common ground between Derrida and Rorty does not preclude the recognition of important differences between their approaches. However, it is to suggest that a fruitful dialogue can be envisaged between them despite – or rather one might say precisely

1

because of – those differences. Such was the aim of the symposium that is at the origin of this volume. Its purpose was to inquire in which way Derridean deconstruction and Rortyian pragmatism could contribute to the elaboration of a non-foundationalist thinking about democracy. The idea was to examine their points of convergence as well as their disagreements in this particular terrain and to discuss their respective insights. For that purpose, we invited two other theorists who have helped to develop the deconstructive approach along slightly different lines: Simon Critchley, who complements it with a Levinasian opening to the ethical experience of the other, and Ernesto Laclau, who has proposed to link deconstruction with the logic of 'hegemony'.

Deconstruction and Politics

Several issues were at stake in the encounter. To begin with, we had to scrutinize the relevance of deconstruction for politics. This could not be taken for granted and it did constitute a moot point in the exchange. Indeed, while celebrating the importance of Derrida as a world-disclosing ironist, Rorty has consistently denied the political implications of his work. According to the distinction between 'private ironist' and 'public liberal', which he proposes in *Contingency, Irony and Solidarity,* Derrida should be seen as a 'private ironist'. His work has no public utility and nothing to contribute to political life in a liberal society.

Such a thesis was examined and rejected by Simon Critchley, who made a claim for the overriding ethical significance of deconstruction. According to Critchley, Derrida should be seen as a public thinker and his work, with its growing emphasis on justice and responsibility, has important ethical and political implications. To be sure, Derrida's conception of justice as an 'experience' of the undecidable[1] cannot be instantiated in the public realm, but that does not mean that it has no consequence for politics. It is Rorty's over-rigid distinction between public and private which blinds him to the complexity of the weaving between the two spheres, and which leads him to denounce any attempt to articulate the quest for individual autonomy with the question of social justice.

Ernesto Laclau, for his part, brought to the fore the relevance for politics of two dimensions of deconstruction: undecidability and decision. In his view, the central theme of deconstruction is the politico-discursive production of society. By showing the structural undecidability of numerous areas of the social, deconstruction reveals the contingency of the social, widening in that way the field of political institution. It is therefore primarily a *political* logic. While compatible with a variety of political strategies, it is particularly important for democratic theory because it permits radicalization of some of its trends and arguments. For Laclau, undecidability and decision are constitutive of the tension which makes possible a political society. However, he argues that in order to produce all its political effects, deconstruction requires a theory of hegemony, i.e. a theory of the decision taken in an undecidable terrain. Only hegemony can help to theorize the distance between structural undecidability and actuality.

Rorty's New Pragmatism

With respect to Rorty's version of pragmatism, the controverted issue was not its relevance for politics, which nobody denies, but the kind of liberal utopia and the piecemeal type of social engineering that it promotes. By insisting on the need to keep completely apart the private and the public realms and by envisaging politics solely in terms of pragmatic, short-term compromises, isn't he missing an important dimension of the democratic vision? Can such a reformism do justice to the multiplicity of struggles which call for a radicalization of the democratic ideal?

Critchley took issue with Rorty's assertion that there is no way to unite or reconcile the public and private domains and that we must come to terms with the fact that we have two irreconciliable final vocabularies: one where the desire for self-creation and autonomy dominates, and another one where what dominates is the desire for community. When he declares that those different vocabularies function in two different languages games, the public and the private, and that it is dangerous to confuse their field of application, Rorty deprives us of the rich critical potential opened by public ironists like Nietzsche and Foucault. Moreover, wonders Critchley, doesn't such a distinction of the self into ironist and liberal create the conditions for political cynicism?

According to Laclau, it is only in a rationalistic world – one clearly at odds with Rorty's anti-foundationalist premises – that the demands of self-realization and those of human solidarity could be so neatly differentiated. In his view, the distinction public/private, important as it is for democratic politics, is not one of essence. It should be problematized and envisaged as an unstable frontier constantly trespassed, with personal autonomy investing public aims and the private becoming politicized. There is therefore no reason to oppose in such a drastic way the private demands for self-creation and the public ones for human solidarity.

To criticize Rorty's politics does not signify, though, that we should renounce pragmatism. While unhappy with the liberal piecemeal politics advocated by Rorty, Laclau points out that he is not calling for a rejection of the pragmatic approach. Indeed, he stresses his agreement with several aspects of the Rortyian outlook, which, he says, is compatible with different types of politics. Pragmatic premises do not necessary lead to the type of liberalism favoured by Rorty and they can, for instance, be articulated with a radical-democratic perspective.

Despite the fact that their arguments did not manage to convince Rorty, it seems to me that both Critchley and Laclau presented, albeit in different ways, a convincing case for the importance of deconstruction for politics. Their views are not, however, entirely convergent. Both of them agree that an argument concerning structural undecidability cannot provide, in and of itself, any positive grounding for a decision and that something else is required. But with respect to the kind of complement that is needed, their positions differ. This something else is found by Critchley in an ethical grounding along Levinasian lines: the radical opening to the other is a primary experience from which normative contents can be derived. For Laclau, on the contrary, this moment of quasi-grounding (the decision) is something akin to a self-grounding which is, however, radically contingent – it points in that sense to a primacy of politics rather than ethics and to a theory of 'hegemony' as the bridge between undecidability and decision.

Democracy and Rationality

One point on which there was an agreement was that, despite the fact that it was impossible to derive one single type of politics from either deconstruction or pragmatism, both approaches could provide important insights for democratic politics. It is on this issue that I want to make a few further comments taking the ensemble of the discussion into account.

Rorty is, I think, most useful when he criticizes the pretensions of Kantian-inspired philosophers like Habermas, who want to find a viewpoint standing above politics from which one could guarantee the superiority of democracy. Surely he is right to assert: 'We should have to abandon the hopeless task of finding politically neutral premises, premises which can be justified to anybody, from which to infer an obligation to pursue democratic politics.'[2] According to Rorty, we have to acknowledge that our democratic and liberal principles define only one possible language game among others. It is then futile to search for arguments in their favour which would not be 'context-dependent' in order to secure them against other political language games.

Against Apel and Habermas, Rorty argues that it is not possible to derive a universalistic moral philosophy from the philosophy of language. There is nothing, for him, in the nature of language that could serve as a basis for justifying to all possible audiences the superiority of liberal democracy. He insists that envisaging democratic advances as if they were linked to progresses in rationality is not helpful, and that we should stop presenting the institutions of liberal Western societies as offering the rational solution to the problem of human coexistence; as the solution that other people will necessarily adopt when they cease being 'irrational'. In his view, what is at stake here has nothing to do with rationality but is a matter of shared beliefs. To call somebody irrational in this context, he states, 'is not to say that she is not making proper use of her mental faculties. It is only to say that she does not seem to share enough beliefs and desires with one to make conversation with her on the disputed point fruitful. So force, rather than persuasion, will have to be used.'[3]

Democratic action, in this perspective, does not require a theory of truth and notions like unconditionality and universal validity but rather a variety of practices and pragmatic moves aimed at persuading people to broaden the range of their commitments to others, to build a more inclusive community. For Rorty, it is through sentiment and sympathy, not through rationality and universalistic moral discourse, that democratic advances take place. This is why he considers books like *Uncle Tom's Cabin* to have played a more important role than philosophical treatises in securing moral progress.

This is certainly a more promising way of thinking about democratic politics and I share Rorty's conviction that it is high time to 'peel apart Enlightenment liberalism from Enlightenment rationalism'.[4] It is particularly important in the present conjuncture, characterized as it is by an increasing disaffection towards democracy, to understand how a strong adhesion to democratic values and institutions can be established and that rationalism constitutes an obstacle to such understanding. It is necessary to realize that it is not by offering sophisticated rational arguments nor by making context-transcendent truth claims about the superiority of liberal democracy that democratic values can be fostered. The creation of democratic forms of individuality is a question of *identification* with democratic values and this is a complex process that takes place through a diversity of practices, discourses and languages games.

This is something that Rortyian pragmatism, with the importance it gives to shared vocabularies, can help us to grasp much better than can universalist and rationalist moral theories. By putting an exclusive emphasis on the arguments needed to secure the *legitimacy* of liberal institutions, recent moral and political philosophy have been asking the wrong question. The real issue is not to find arguments to justify the rationality or universality of liberal democracy that would be acceptable by every rational or reasonable person. Liberal democratic principles can only be defended in a contextualist manner, as being constitutive of our form of life, and we should not try to ground our commitment to them on something supposedly safer. To secure allegiance and adhesion to those principles what is needed is the creation of a democratic *ethos*. It has to do with the mobilization of passions and sentiments, the multiplication of practices, institutions and languages games that provide the conditions of possibility for democratic subjects and democratic forms of willing.

Most liberal theorists are bound to miss the relevance of that kind of reflection because they operate with a metaphysical conception which sees the individual as prior to society, bearer of natural rights, utility maximizer or rational subject – according to the brand of liberalism that they follow – but, in all cases, as abstracted from social and power relations, language, culture and the whole set of practices that make agency possible. Indeed, what is precluded in all those approaches is the crucial question of how is democratic agency possible; what are the conditions of existence of the liberal democratic subject?

Against the type of liberalism that searches for universal rational justification and believes that democratic institutions would be more stable if it could be proven that they would be chosen by rational individuals under the veil of ignorance or in a situation of undistorted communication, Rorty's pragmatism reminds us of the limits of the claims of reason. By urging us to think in term of practices, it compels us to confront the real issues that have to be tackled in order to enhance democratic citizenship.

Philosophy, Politics and Democracy

However, once Rorty's important contribution has been acknowledged, the shortcomings of his approach also need to be pointed out. Like Critchley and Laclau, I have serious reservations with respect to his liberal utopia and the dangers of complacency that it entails. I want to suggest that the basic problem lies in the fact that Rorty does not fully acknowledge the complexity of politics and that this is linked to his dismissal of any kind of theoretical inquiry into the nature of the political realm. For him, politics is 'a matter of pragmatic, short-term reforms and compromises.[15] It is something to be deliberated about in banal, familiar terms'.

The enemies of human happiness in his view are greed, sloth and hypocrisy and no deep analysis is required to understand how they could be eliminated. What 'we liberals' should aim at is to create the largest possible consensus among people about the worth of liberal institutions. What is needed is a bigger dose of liberalism – which he defines in terms of encouraging tolerance and minimizing suffering – and a growing number of liberal societies. Democratic politics is only a matter of letting an increasing number of people count as members of our moral and conversational 'we'. Like his hero John Dewey, Rorty's understanding of social conflict is limited because he is unable to come to terms with the implications of value pluralism and accept that the conflict between fundamental values can never be resolved. He hopes that with economic growth and the development of more tolerant attitudes, harmony can finally be established.

It is for that reason that he cannot see the utility of the kind of quasi-transcendental reflection carried out by Derrida about 'infra-structures'.

For him, Derridean notions like 'supplementarity', 'arche-trace', '*différ-ance*', 'iterability', 're-mark' have no relevance whatsoever for democratic politics. By allowing us to take our distance with such metaphysical questioning, pragmatism, or so Rorty believes, provides us with a stand-point from which to achieve contact with real political issues.

But to affirm that democracy cannot have – and does not need – philosophical foundations is one thing. It is quite another to reject the usefulness of any kind of philosophical reflection and to believe that it has no purchase on an inquiry into the nature of democracy and that we can do without it. Any conception of democratic politics, even one apparently so anti-philosophical as that advocated by Rorty, necessarily entails a certain understanding of the nature of politics. It also implies privileging one of the various meanings of such a contested concept as 'democracy'. There is no neutral ground, supposedly uncontaminated by philosophy, from which to speak.

Oddly enough, when we examine Rorty's unacknowledged presupposi-tions about politics and democracy, we find that he is – with his insistence on dialogue and conversation – more akin to Habermas that one would have expected. Both of them, for instance, envisage moral and political progress in terms of the universalization of the liberal democratic model. The difference consists in the fact that, while Habermas believes that such a process will take place through rational argumentation and that it requires arguments from transculturally valid premises for the superiority of Western liberalism, Rorty pins his hope on persuasion and economic progress. Since, for him, democracy is basically a question of people becoming 'nicer' to one another and behaving in a more tolerant way, he imagines that everything depends on people having more secure con-ditions of existence and sharing more beliefs and desires with others. Hence his conviction that through economic growth and the right kind of 'sentimental education', a wide consensus could be construed around liberal institutions.

The basic difference between the two approaches concerns the different ways in which they envisage the creation of the liberal consensus. Rorty declares, for instance, 'The pragmatists' justification of toleration, free enquiry, and the quest for undistorted communication can only take the form of a comparison between societies which exemplify those habits and those which do not, leading up to the suggestion that nobody who has experienced both would prefer the latter.'[6] It is clear therefore that what he finds unsatisfactory in Habermas is not the latter's quest for undistorted communication but the way in which he pursues it.

This is, of course, not a small matter and I have already indicated that I find Rorty's approach more adequate. The problem, in my view, resides in what he shares with Habermas, or I should rather say, in what is lacking in both of them. Indeed, neither of them is able to grasp the crucial role of conflict and the central integrative function that it plays in a pluralist democracy. This is why they end up proposing what can be called a 'consensus' view of democracy.

What they sweep away with such a move is a very important dimension of democratic politics. Indeed, the specificity of liberal democracy as a new political form of society consists in the legitimation of conflict and the refusal to eliminate it through the imposition of an authoritarian order. A liberal democracy is above all a *pluralist* democracy. Its novelty resides in its envisaging the diversity of conceptions of the good, not as something negative that should be suppressed, but as something to be valued and celebrated. This requires the presence of institutions that establish a specific dynamic between consensus and dissent. Consensus, of course, is necessary, but it should be limited to the institutions that are constitutive of the democratic order. A pluralist democracy needs also to make room for the expression of dissent and for conflicting interests and values. And those should not be seen as temporary obstacles on the road to consensus since in their absence democracy would cease to be pluralistic. This is why democratic politics cannot aim towards harmony and reconciliation. To believe that a final resolution of conflict is eventually possible, even when it is envisaged as asymptotic approaching to the regulative idea of a free unconstrained communication, as in Habermas, is to put the pluralist democratic project at risk.

Indeed, one cannot take seriously the existence of a plurality of legitimate values without recognizing that they will conflict. And this conflict cannot be visualized merely in terms of competing interests that could be adjudicated or accommodated without any form of violence. Many conflicts are antagonistic because they take place among conflicting interpretations of the ethico-political values embodied in liberal democratic institutions. The progress of democracy, *pace* Rorty, will never take the form of a smooth, progressive evolution in which the 'we liberals' get bigger and more inclusive as more and more rights are being recognized. Rights will conflict and no vibrant democratic life can exist without a real democratic confrontation among conflicting rights and without a challenge to existing power relations.

Politics, especially democratic politics, can never overcome conflict and division. Its aim is to establish unity in a context of conflict and diversity; it is concerned with the formation of a 'we' as opposed to a 'them'. What is specific of democratic politics is not the overcoming of the we/them opposition but the different way in which it is drawn. This is why grasping the nature of democratic politics requires a coming to terms with the dimension of antagonism that is present in social relations.

This antagonistic dimension – which I have proposed to designate as *the political*[7] – is precisely what the consensus approach is unable to acknowledge. This distinction is overlooked by rationalists like Habermas, because their conception of democracy must postulate the availability of a consensus without exclusion, i.e. a consensus that is the expression of a rational agreement and that would have completely eliminated antagonism. It is also neglected by others like Rorty (but this is also true for Rawls), because their strong separation between the public and the private leads them to the mistaken belief that disagreements might be relegated to the private and an overlapping consensus created in the public sphere. In both cases, the result is the same: a conception of the well-ordered democratic society as free from antagonism and without exclusion – in order words, the illusion that it is possible to establish a 'we' that would not imply the existence of a 'them'.

Deconstruction and Democracy

This privileging of the 'consensus' with the different forms that it currently takes in the numerous versions of 'deliberative democracy' represents in my view a serious misconception of the nature of democracy. This is why an approach like deconstruction, which reveals the impossibility of establishing a consensus without exclusion is of fundamental importance for grasping what is at stake in democratic politics. Because it warns us against the illusion that Justice could ever be instantiated in the institutions of any society, deconstruction forces us to keep the democratic contestation alive. By pointing to the ineradicability of antagonism, notions like undecidability and decision are not only fundamental for politics, as Laclau indicates, they also provide the very terrain in which a democratic pluralist politics can be formulated.

As Derrida stresses, without taking a rigorous account of undecidability, it is impossible to think the concepts of political decision and ethical responsibility. Undecidability is not a moment to be traversed or overcome and conflicts of duty are interminable. I can never be completely satisfied that I have made a good choice since a decision in favour of one alternative is always to the detriment of another one. It is in that sense that deconstruction can be said to be 'hyperpoliticizing'. Politicization never ceases because undecidability continues to inhabit the decision. Every consensus appears as a stabilization of something essentially unstable and chaotic. Chaos and instability are irreducible, but as Derrida indicates, this is at once a risk and a chance, since continual stability would mean the end of politics and ethics.

If Rorty shares with Habermas a view of politics that puts too much emphasis on consensus, deconstruction's problematizing of the very idea of consensus dovetails with several aspects of the approach of Stanley Cavell. In his critique of John Rawls in the Carus Lectures, for instance, Cavell points out that Rawls's account of justice omits a very important dimension of what takes places when we assess the claims made upon us in the name of justice in situations in which it is the degree of society's compliance with its ideal that is in question. He takes issue with Rawls's assertion that, 'Those who express resentment must be prepared to show why certain institutions are unjust or how others have injured them.'[8] In Rawls's view, if they are unable to do so, we can consider that our conduct is above reproach and bring the conversation on justice to an end. But, asks Cavell, 'what if there is a cry of justice that expresses a sense not of having lost out in an unequal yet fair struggle, but of having from the start being left out?'[9] Giving as example the situation of Nora in Ibsen's play *A Doll's House*, he shows how deprivation of a voice in the conversation of justice can be the work of the moral consensus itself. He urges us to realize that bringing a conversation to a close is always a personal choice, it is a *decision* which cannot be simply presented as a mere application of procedures and justified as the only move that we could make in those circumstances. Of course, such a decision can be justified in certain cases but we should never refuse bearing responsibility for our decision by invoking the commands of general rules or principles.

If Rawls were to take Cavell's objection seriously, he would have to abandon the idea that justice could ever be instantiated in a well-ordered society. Alas, his recent writing has not followed that path and the distinction that he now establishes between 'simple pluralism' and 'reasonable pluralism' goes in the opposite direction. Indeed, it allows him to exclude from the conversation on justice all of those who do not agree with the liberal premises, while presenting this political decision as a moral requirement, product of the 'free exercise of democratic public reason'. An even more drastic way to silence the voice of those who disagree with the dominant consensus and to allow for the possibility of liberals feeling 'beyond reproach'.[10]

When we accept that every consensus exists as a temporary result of a provisional hegemony, as a stabilization of power, and that it always entails some form of exclusion, we can begin to envisage democratic politics in a different way. A democratic approach which, thanks to the insights of deconstruction, is able to acknowledge the real nature of its frontiers and recognizes the forms of exclusion that they embody, instead of trying to disguise them under the veil of rationality or morality, can help us to fight against the dangers of complacency. Since it is aware of the fact that difference is the condition of possibility of constituting unity and totality at the same time that it provides its essential limits, such an approach can contribute to subverting the ever-present temptation that exists in democratic societies to naturalize their frontiers and essentialize their identities. For that reason, a project of 'radical and plural democracy' informed by deconstruction will be more receptive to the multiplicity of voices that a pluralist society encompasses and to the complexity of the power structure that this network of differences implies. Indeed, it will be able to understand that the specificity of modern pluralist democracy resides not in the absence of oppression and violence but in the presence of the institutions that permit these aspects to be limited and contested. And therefore it will be more likely to ask how those institutions could be multiplied and enhanced.

Democratic politics cannot do without philosophical reflection because in order to understand its own dynamics, it needs to draw all the consequences of the fact that power and antagonism are ineradicable. But this is precisely what is made impossible when some exclusions are presented as the expression of the 'free exercise of public reason'. Hence the importance of the deconstructive approach and its superiority over all those who aim at consensus. In order to impede the closure of the democratic space, it is vital to abandon any reference to the possibility of a consensus that, because it would be grounded on justice or on rationality, could not be destabilized. To believe in the possibility of such a consensus, even when it is conceived as an 'infinite task', is to postulate that harmony and reconciliation should be the goal of a democratic society. In other words, it is to transform the pluralist democratic ideal into a 'self-refuting ideal', since the very moment of its realization would coincide with its destruction. As conditions of possibility for the existence of a pluralist democracy, conflicts and antagonisms constitute at the same time the condition of impossibility of its final achievement. Such is the 'double bind' that deconstruction unveils. This is why, in Derrida's words, democracy will always be 'to come', traversed by undecidability and for ever keeping open its element of promise.

Notes

1 It is important to stress here that Critchley refers to Derrida's conception of justice as 'an "experience" of the undecidable' and not as an experience of the 'unexperiencable' as Rorty says in his answer to Critchley. This is quite different.

2 Rorty, Richard, 'Sind Aussagen universelle Geltungsanspruche?', *Deutsche Zeitschrift für Philosophie*, no. 6, 1994, p. 986.

3 Rorty, Richard, 'Justice as a Larger Loyalty', paper presented at the Seventh East–West Philosophers' Conference, University of Hawaii, January 1995, mimeographed, p. 20.

4 Ibid., p. 22.

5 Rorty, Richard, 'Remarks on Deconstruction and Pragmatism', in this volume, p. 17.

6 Rorty, Richard, *Objectivity, Relativism and Truth*, Cambridge, Cambridge University Press, 1991, p. 29.

7 See in this respect Mouffe, Chantal, *The Return of The Political*, London, Verso, 1993.

8 Rawls, John, *A Theory of Justice*, Cambridge, Mass., Harvard University Press, 1971, p. 533.

9 Cavell, Stanley, *Conditions Handsome and Unhandsome*, Chicago, Chicago University Press, 1990, p. xxxviii.
10 This distinction between 'simple pluralism' and 'reasonable pluralism' is elaborated by Rawls in *Political Liberalism*, New York, Columbia University Press, 1993. For a detailed critique of its implications see: Chantal Mouffe, 'Democracy and Pluralism: A Critique of the Rationalist Approach', *Cardozo Law Review*, vol. 16, no. 5, March 1995.

2

Remarks on Deconstruction and Pragmatism

Richard Rorty

Derrida is read, by conservative know-nothings in the United States and Britain, as a frivolous and cynical despiser of common sense and traditional democratic values. Many of my colleagues in the Anglophone philosophical community support this reading, and attempt to excommunicate Derrida from the philosophical profession.

Derrida is read by his fans in American departments of literature, on the other hand, as the philosopher who has transformed our notions of language and the self. They think of him as having demonstrated the truth of certain important propositions, propositions the recognition of which undermines our traditional ways of understanding ourselves, and understanding the books we read. They also take him to have given us a method – the deconstructive method – of reading texts: a method which helps us see what these texts are really about, what is really going on in them.

I find both these ways of reading Derrida equally dubious, and I shall discuss them in turn.

I think that the first misreading has been made easier by the fact that, due to an accident of timing and the necessities of popular journalism, Derrida and Foucault have been bracketed together, and labelled 'French post-structuralism'. These two original thinkers seem to me to have very little in common, apart from their shared Nietzschean suspicions about the tradition of Western philosophy – suspicions which they share with the American pragmatists.[1]

The big difference between Foucault and Derrida is that Derrida is a sentimental, hopeful, romantically idealistic writer. Foucault, on the other hand, often seems to be doing his best to have no social hope and no human feelings. One cannot imagine Derrida hoping to write 'so as to have no face', any more than one can imagine Nietzsche doing so. Despite his prediction that 'the Book' will be replaced by 'the text', Derrida intensely admires the great authors who stand behind the texts he glosses; he has

13

no doubts about his or their authorship. Although he of course has doubts about metaphysical accounts of the nature of the self and of writing, he has no interest in dissolving the books in which great human imaginations have been most fully themselves into anonymous, rootless, free-floating 'discourses'.

Whereas Foucault cultivates aloofness, Derrida throws himself into the arms of the texts he writes about. Cynical detachment is not the whole story about Foucault, but it is an irreplaceable part of that story. Yet it has no part in any plausible story about Derrida – any more than does frivolity. When, in the past, I have described Derrida as 'playful', this has sometimes been read as a dismissive epithet – suggesting that there is something lightweight about him. But I would use the same adjective of Plato and Nietzsche, and in the same sense. There is a difference between 'play' in the approbative sense in which Schiller used it – to say, for example, that man is fully human only when he plays – and what the know-nothings mean by 'frivolity'.

I turn now to the misreading of Derrida by his Anglophone fans. I think it very unfortunate that Derrida's fans describe him as criticizing *humanism*. 'Humanism' can mean a certain Platonic-Cartesian-Kantian account of what it is to be human. But it can also mean, and to the untutored it typically conveys, participation in the hopes of the Enlightenment – and specifically the hope that human beings, once they have set God and the various surrogates for God to one side, may learn to rely on their own romantic imagination, and their own ability to cooperate with each other for the common good.

In this latter sense, Derrida seems to me as good a humanist as Mill or Dewey. When Derrida talks about deconstruction as prophetic of 'the democracy that is to come', he seems to me to be expressing the same utopian social hope as was felt by these earlier dreamers. When he says that he yearns for a time when man and woman can be friends – a time when we have got beyond the 'virile homosexuality' which is entwined with phallogocentric metaphysics – he seems to me to be expressing the same sort of utopian hope. The interweaving of these two themes in his essay 'The Politics of Friendship' makes that very moving text one of my own favourites.

His Anglophone fans typically use Derrida for the same purposes as Marx and Freud have long been used by literary critics. They think of him as providing new, improved tools for unmasking books and authors – showing what is really going on behind a false front. I do not think that a critic of metaphysics, in the tradition of Nietzsche and Heidegger, should be read in this way. For without the traditional concepts of metaphysics one cannot make sense of the appearance–reality distinction, and without that distinction one cannot make sense of the notion of 'what is really going on'. No more metaphysics, no more unmasking.

These fans also think that there is a method called 'deconstruction' which one can apply to texts and teach to students. I have never been able to figure out what this method is, nor what was being taught to students except some such maxim like 'Find something that can be made to look self-contradictory, claim that that contradiction is the central message of the text, and ring some changes on it.' Application of this maxim produced, in the 1970s and 1980s, tens of thousands of 'deconstructive readings' of texts by American and British professors – readings which were as formulaic and as boring as the tens of thousands of readings which resulted from dutifully applying the maxim 'Find something that can be made to sound like a symptom of an unresolved Oedipus complex.'

This flurry of deconstructive activity seems to me to have added little to our understanding of literature and to have done little for leftist politics. On the contrary, by diverting attention from real politics, it has helped create a self-satisfied and insular academic left which – like the left of the 1960s – prides itself on not being co-opted by the system and thereby renders itself less able to improve the system. Irving Howe's much-quoted jibe – 'These people don't want to take over the government; they just want to take over the English Department' – seems to me to remain an important criticism of this academic left.

I see no real connection between what Derrida is up to and the activity which is called 'deconstruction', and I wish that the latter word had never taken hold as a description of Derrida's work. I have never found, or been able to invent, a satisfactory definition of that word. I often use it as shorthand for 'the sort of thing Derrida does', but I do so *faute de mieux*, and with a self-exculpatory shrug. In an article called 'Deconstruction' (published in volume 8 of *The Cambridge History of Literary Criticism*), I claim that there are deep differences between Derrida's own motives and interests and those of Paul de Man, the founder of the school of literary criticism which was briefly (before the advent of 'cultural studies') dominant in the US. I argue that the de Manian way of reading texts – as testifying to 'the presence of a nothingness' – is very different from Derrida's approach to texts.

So much for the opposed misreadings of Derrida which I mentioned at the outset. I turn now to the relation of the sort of thing that Derrida does to pragmatism.

Pragmatism starts out from Darwinian naturalism – from a picture of human beings as chance products of evolution. This starting-point leads pragmatists to be as suspicious of the great binary oppositions of Western metaphysics as are Heidegger and Derrida. Darwinians share Nietzschean suspicions of Platonic other-worldliness, and the Nietzschean conviction that distinctions like mind-vs.-body and objective-vs.-subjective need to be reformulated in order to cleanse them of Platonic presuppositions and give them a firmly naturalistic sense. Naturalists, like Derrideans, have no use for what Derrida calls 'a full presence which is beyond play', and they distrust, as much as he does, the various God-surrogates which have been proposed for the role of such a full presence. Both kinds of philosophers see everything as constituted by its relations to other things, and as having no intrinsic, ineluctable nature. What it is depends on what it is being related to (or, if you like, what it differs from).

When it comes to language, pragmatists see the later Wittgenstein, Quine and Davidson as having got rid of the dualistic, Fregean ways of thinking which dominated the *Tractatus Logico-Philosophicus* and early analytic philosophy. They read Derrida on language as making pretty much the same criticisms of the Cartesian/Lockean/Husserlian view of 'language as the expression of thought' which Wittgenstein made in his *Philosophical Investigations*. They read both Derrida and Wittgenstein not as having discovered the essential nature of language, or of anything else, but simply as having helped get rid of a misleading, and useless, picture – the one which Quine called the myth of the museum: the image of there being an object, the meaning, and next to it its label, the word.

What pragmatists find most foreign in Derrida is his suspicion of empiricism, and naturalism – his assumption that these are forms of metaphysics, rather than replacements for metaphysics. To put it another way: they cannot understand why Derrida wants to sound *transcendental*, why he persists in taking the project of finding conditions of possibility seriously. So when pragmatists are told by 'deconstructionists' that Derrida has 'demonstrated' that Y, the condition of the possibility of X, is also the condition of the impossibility of X, they feel that this is an unnecessarily high-faluting way of putting a point which could be put a lot more simply: viz., that you cannot use the word 'A' without being able to use the word 'B', and vice versa, even though nothing can be both an A and an B.

In my own writing about Derrida I have urged that we see him as sharing Dewey's utopian hopes, but not treat his work as contributing, in any clear or direct way, to the realization of those hopes. I divide philosophers, rather crudely, into those (like Mill, Dewey and Rawls) whose work fulfils primarily public purposes, and those whose work fulfils primarily private purposes. I think of the Nietzsche–Heidegger–Derrida assault on metaphysics as producing private satisfactions to people who are deeply involved with philosophy (and therefore, necessarily, with metaphysics) but not as politically consequential, except in a very indirect and long-term way. So I think of Derrida as at his best in works like the 'Envois' section of *La Carte postale* – works in which his private relationships to his two grandfathers, Freud and Heidegger, are clearest.

Whereas his Anglophone followers typically read books like *De la grammatologie* as demonstrating philosophical, transcendental truths, I see them as propaedeutic. Derrida's earlier, less idiosyncratic, more 'strictly philosophical' work – and in particular his books on Husserl – were necessary to get him a hearing, necessary to establish himself and get himself published. But, although I find these works very valuable, I do not read them as 'contributions to philosophy', in the sense of books that demonstrate, now and forever, certain theses. I read them as books in which Derrida works out his private relationships to the figures who have meant most to him. I prefer texts like 'Envois' and 'Circonfession' because these seem to me more vivid and forceful forms of private self-creation than is possible through the explication of texts, even when this explication is exceptionally brilliant and original.

Because I read my favourite Derridean texts in this way, I have trouble with the specifically Levinasian strains in his thought. In particular, I am unable to connect Levinas's pathos of the infinite with ethics or politics. I see ethics and politics – real politics as opposed to cultural politics – as a matter of reaching accommodation between competing interests, and as something to be deliberated about in banal, familiar terms – terms which do not need philosophical dissection and do not have philosophical presuppositions.

When Dewey talked politics, as opposed to doing philosophy, he offered advice about how to avoid getting hung up on traditional ways of doing things, how to redescribe the situation in terms which might facilitate compromise, and how to take fairly small, reformist steps. Levinas's pathos of the infinite chimes with radical, revolutionary politics, but not with reformist, democratic politics – which is, I think, the only sort of politics needed in rich constitutional democracies such as Britain, France and the US.

To conclude, I see romantic and utopian hopes of the sort developed in 'The Politics of Friendship' as a contribution to Derrida's private self-fashioning, and thus to that of some of his readers (including, obviously, myself). But I do not see texts such as 'The Politics of Friendship' as contributions to political thought. Politics, as I see it, is a matter of pragmatic, short-term reforms and compromises – compromises which must, in a democratic society, be proposed and defended in terms much less esoteric than those in which we overcome the metaphysics of presence. Political thought centres on the attempt to formulate some hypotheses about how, and under what conditions, such reforms might be effected. I want to save radicalism and pathos for private moments, and stay reformist and pragmatic when it comes to my dealings with other people.

Note

1 The assimilation of pragmatism to Nietzsche seems to shock people, but it was made very early on. See René Berthelot, *Un romantisme utilitaire: étude sur le*

mouvement pragmatiste, vol. 1, *Le Pragmatisme chez Nietzsche et chez Poincare*, Paris, Felix Alcan, 1911. Berthelot, whose paradigm of pragmatism is William James, refers to Nietzsche as 'un pragmatiste allemand'.

3

Deconstruction and Pragmatism – Is Derrida a Private Ironist or a Public Liberal?

Simon Critchley

Introduction

Is pragmatism deconstructive? Is deconstruction pragmatist? At a super-ficial level, the response to the first question is clearly affirmative, in so far as pragmatism deconstructs all forms of foundationalism (Platonism, Metaphysical Realism, Analytic Neo-Kantianism, Pre-Heideggerian Phen-omenology), and argues for the contingency of language, self and com-munity. The pragmatist deconstructs the epistemological picture of truth as a glassy correspondence or clear and distinct representation between the mind and external reality, and replaces it with the claim that truth is what it is good to believe (James) or whatever one is warranted in asserting (Dewey). With regard to the second question, it can perhaps be said that deconstruction is pragmatist in two senses: first, that the deconstruction of texts from the history of philosophy (e.g. Plato, Rousseau or Husserl) in terms of the detection of what Derrida calls 'the metaphysics of presence' can be assimilated to an anti-foundationalist critique of philo-sophy; second, that the deconstructive claim that the ideality of meaning is an effect of the differential constitution of language, what Derrida calls the general text or, more helpfully, context, can be assimilated to a pragmatist conception of meaning as a function of context, i.e. the Wittgensteinian reduction of meaning to use (Rorty 1991b, p. 125).

So, at this superficial level, it would indeed seem that pragmatism is deconstructive and deconstruction is pragmatist. Yet, is this the whole story? In this chapter, I would like to disrupt this identification of deconstruction with pragmatism from the perspective of Derrida's work, and raise some critical questions about Rorty's understanding of decon-struction, particularly as this impinges on questions of ethics and politics. Thus, if I admit at the outset that deconstruction is allied to pragmatism, then the question is whether *deconstruction is pragmatist all the way down?*

That is to say, is deconstruction consistently anti-foundationalist? Or is there a foundationalist claim in deconstruction which cannot be pragmatized: justice, for example, or reponsibility to another's suffering? As we will see presently, this is the same question as to whether Derrida is *only* a private ironist, calling us to recognize the utter contingency of the philosophical tradition, a tradition that we are now in a position to circumvent (a favourite verb of Rorty's in his discussions of Derrida), and where Derrida's work functions as an exemplar of the forms of autonomy and individual perfection that might be available to anyone in a utopian liberal society.

In texts like the 'Envois' to *La Carte postale*, which is Rorty's prime example of what interests him in deconstruction, Derrida is clearly an ironist, in particular he ironizes about the validity or univocity of Heidegger's account of the history of Being.[1] But, is Derrida *only* an ironist? That is to say, in Rorty's vocabulary, is it not also possible for Derrida to be a liberal? For Rorty, Derrida can only be understood as a private thinker whose work has no public utility and therefore no interesting ethical or political consequences. Concealed in this claim is, I believe, a normative belief to the effect that Derrida *should* not be considered as a public thinker. The reason for this is that Rorty believes if Derrida's work were extended into the public realm, then this would produce either useless, pernicious or possibly even *dangerous* ethical and political consequences. When Rorty discusses the question of the public significance of deconstruction, Derrida tends to get tarred with the same brush as Heidegger: namely, that Heidegger, for Rorty, is the most sublime theoretical imagination of his time (Rorty 1989, p. 118), just as Derrida is the most ingenious and imaginative of contemporary philosophers (Rorty forthcoming, p. 2), and just what one needs if one has felt the power of Heidegger's language but one does not want to describe oneself in terms of that language. However, Heidegger's work – and *a fortiori* Derrida's work – has no public utility; that is, it has no role in the political life of liberal society. Therefore, Derrida is a private ironist. Against this conclusion, I will try to show how, in Rorty's terms, it is possible both for Derrida to be a public liberal and for deconstruction to have overriding ethical and political consequences.

Rorty's Later Work: Presentation and Critique

To approach this issue, we need to define some terms and establish the general framework for Rorty's pragmatism. As a proviso, let me say that I will be restricting my discussion of Rorty to *Contingency, Irony and Solidarity* (Rorty 1989), to the reading of Derrida given therein and in some papers contemporary with and prior to that book.[2]

For Rorty, the liberal (and Rorty always personifies the positions he describes – 'the liberal ironist', 'the pragmatist' – which adds a helpful dramatic quality to the writing, but sometimes has the negative effect of reducing these positions to caricatures) is someone who believes that cruelty is the worst thing that there is. Liberal society, therefore, must encourage the value of tolerance as a way of minimizing suffering. The ironist is someone who faces up to the contingency of their most central beliefs and desires – beliefs about the nature of language, the self and community and desires for autonomy and perfection. The heroine (Rorty always uses the feminine gender to describe the position he is advocating, whereas the liberal metaphysician – let's call him Habermas or the early Rawls – is always gendered male) of *Contingency, Irony and Solidarity* is the figure of the liberal ironist, someone who is committed to social justice and appalled by cruelty, but who recognizes that there is no metaphysical foundation to her concern for justice.

However, the core of Rorty's analysis – which has been the object of much hostile critical attention – is the distinction between the public and the private. It is important to point out that this distinction is not the Hellenistic or Arendtian demarcation of *oikos* and *polis*, between the domestic hearth and the public forum. The private is defined by Rorty as being concerned 'with idiosyncratic projects of self-overcoming', with self-creation and the pursuit of autonomy. The public is defined as being concerned with those activities 'having to do with the suffering of other human beings', with the attempt to minimize cruelty and work for social justice (Rorty forthcoming, p. 1). Rorty's central claim in *Contingency, Irony and Solidarity* – a claim, moreover, that would be devastating to much work in philosophy if taken seriously – is that it is theoretically impossible to unite or reconcile the public and private domains. Such a desire for reconciliation lies at the basis of Platonism, Christianity, Kantianism and Marxism (other examples could be given), in so far as each of these has attempted to fuse the claims of self-interest, self-realization, personal salvation or individual autonomy with the *eidos* of justice, charity and love of one's fellow humans, the universality of the categorical imperative or the proletariat as the universal class and agent of history. The dominant legacy of the Platonist tradition is the attempt to reconcile private, individual autonomy with the public good of the community by erecting both upon a common philosophical foundation.

Rorty cuts the Gordian knot in which philosophy has long been entangled, between moral optimists like Kant, who claim that self-realization coincides with a commitment to human solidarity (the tie that binds individual autonomy, the moral law and the kingdom of ends), and moral sceptics like Nietzsche and Freud, who would claim that the desire for human solidarity dissimulates either the will-to-power or libidinal drives. After Hegel – that is to say, for Rorty, after the historical turn in philosophy which coincides with a recognition of contingency, the idea that truth is something created rather than discovered – this contest between moral optimists and moral sceptics becomes a conflict between two forms of historicism. On the one hand, there are historicists for whom the desire for self-creation and autonomy dominates (for Rorty: Foucault and Heidegger), and on the other hand, there are historicists for whom the desire for community dominates and who see the emphasis on self-creation as 'aestheticism' or 'irrationalism' (for Rorty: Dewey and Habermas). Rorty insists that there is no way of reconciling theoretically these two forms of historicism, 'there is no way to bring self-creation together with justice at the level of theory' (Rorty 1989, p. xiv). We must reconcile ourselves to the fact that we have two irreconcilable final vocabularies, which function well in two different language games: the public and the private. To confuse the field of application for each of these two vocabularies would be to engage in a form of category mistake: on the one hand, to judge the public by the standards of the private gives rise to the kind of dangerous errors of which Heidegger was guilty in 1933; on the other hand, to judge the private by the standards of the public produces the kind of myopic readings of Heidegger and Derrida to be found in Habermas's *Philosophical Discourse of Modernity.*

For Rorty, the best that can be hoped for is a person – she, the liberal ironist – who would be able to discriminate public questions from private concerns, questions about cruelty and social justice from concerns about the significance of human life and the quest for autonomy. The liberal ironist would be the sort of person who would be able to distinguish properly the public from the private. Does such a person or community of persons exist? This question allows us to introduce the *utopian* or *critical* element in Rorty's account. Most of the citizens of 'the rich North Atlantic democracies', for reasons of either religious belief or a vague, residual attachment to the humanistic values of the Enlightenment, are liberal metaphysicians. Such people are genuinely concerned with social justice, and they believe that there is one, final moral vocabulary – Christian love, classical liberalism, liberties underwritten by tradition – for deciding political questions, a vocabulary in touch with our essential humanity, our nature. On the other hand, although clearly outnumbered by the meta-physicians, there are non-liberal ironists who are concerned with their self-realization, and perhaps the realization of a small group, but who have no concern for traditional liberal questions of social justice. The critical, utopian function of *Contingency, Irony and Solidarity* is to persuade liberal metaphysicians to become ironists (or at least common-sensical nomin-alists and historicists – Rorty 1989, p. 87) and non-liberal ironists to become liberals. It is important to point out that Rorty believes that such per-suasion will take place not through argument (as in philosophy) but through the *redescriptions* of metaphysics as irony, and of irony as consistent with liberalism. *Contingency, Irony and Solidarity* does not therefore belong to the genre of philosophy, but rather to literary criticism, which, for Rorty, is the only form of discourse that could be of moral relevance in our post-philosophical culture (Rorty 1982, p. 82) – liberal democracy needs literature not philosophy.

Rorty's utopia is the vision of a society of liberal ironists, and progress towards such a utopia will be achieved by the *universalization* (Rorty 1989, p. xv) of liberal society. The obvious (if banal) question to be raised here is how such a commitment to universality can be consistent with Rorty's anti-foundational 'relativism' (between quotation marks, for I take it that relativism would be the name of a pseudo-problem for Rorty). To respond to this, it has to be understood that progress towards this liberal ironic utopia itself depends upon Wilfrid Sellars's analysis of moral obligation, where the universality of a moral vocabulary – that of the liberal in this case – is dependent upon it being shared by a certain community with a similar set of moral intentions: 'we-intentions' (Rorty 1989, pp. 194–8). Thus, our moral vocabulary – that of 'we liberals' – is valid for us, for a community that sees the world the way that we do, as 'we Americans' or 'we citizens of the rich North Atlantic democracies'. Thus, progress towards Rorty's utopia will be achieved by the progressive expansion of the frontiers of liberal democracies, a globalization of Western liberalism.

Of course, it would perhaps be too easy, but none the less still justified, to point towards the evidence of imperialism, racism and colonialism that has always accompanied – or perhaps has always been the reality behind the cynical veneer of a legitimating discourse – the expansionism of Western liberal democracy. Rorty's definition of liberalism is ethico/political and pays no attention to the *economic* liberalism – freedom defined in terms of free markets – which is indeed in the process of rapidly and violently globalizing itself, more often than not without an accompanying commitment to tolerance and the abhorrence of cruelty (for example, China is successfully establishing itself as an economically liberal and politically non-liberal state). Following C.B. Macpherson's classic analysis, it is evident that the historical basis for the development of liberal democracy was a liberal state committed to both a competitive party political system and a competitive market economy, on to which was eventually grafted, after much struggle and bloodshed, a universal democratic franchise.[3] The important point to grasp here is that liberalism denotes an ecomonic as well as a political form of society and there is nothing *necessarily* democratic about the economically liberal state.

But perhaps we are all liberals now. Perhaps the best we can hope for, politically speaking, is a gradualist, reformist approach to politics that will perhaps (and only perhaps) bring about a beautiful liberal society; all sublime dreams of revolutionary transformation seem either hopelessly inadequate or merely quaint. Perhaps Rorty is right to insist that the only response to objective political stagnation is the privatization of the sublimity that radicals had come to expect from politics between 1789 and

1968. Perhaps Rorty is also right to call for a banalization of leftist political language and a subordination of the claims of radical social theory to the facticity of democratic politics, which would entail less *Ideologie-Kritik* and more social criticism of the kind that Rorty finds in Orwell and which can be seen in the best investigative journalism. Perhaps philosophy should be only an underlabourer to democracy, criticizing any drift towards reactionary political movements, intolerance and cruelty and attempting to hegemonize the radical potentialities within liberalism. None the less, I am much less happy about the *tone* of Rorty's statement that 'the rich democracies of the present day already contain the sorts of institutions necessary to their reform' (Rorty forthcoming, p. 21). Such remarks risk political complacency and can be read as a (re)descriptive apologetics for the inequality, intolerance, exploitation and disenfranchisement within actually existing liberal democracies. As Hilary Putnam has recently pointed out in a spirited defence of Dewey's radical democratic politics, 'the democracy that we have is not something to be spurned, but also not something to be satisfied with'.[4] The problem that is caught sight of here, as pointed out by Mark Warren,[5] is that Rorty's purportedly post-philosophical reconstruction of liberalism risks repeating the exhausted abstractions of classical liberalism, against which the left-Hegelian and socialist critiques of liberalism are still largely valid.

I would like to conclude this section with four critical questions connected to the above remarks. First, the question of irony and the public realm. As William Connolly points out,[6] by restricting irony and ironists to the private sphere, Rorty might be said to refuse the possibility of a critique of liberal society that would use the strategy of public irony to uncover the violence that liberalism does so much to try and dissimulate. A recent example of this would be some of the post-Nietzschean readings of the Gulf War, in terms of exposing liberalism's Janus face: one side turned towards legitimacy and universality, i.e. the mechanisms of the United Nations, and the other side turned towards the particularity of violence and war motivated by economic self-interest.[7] Rorty refuses the rich critical potential of seeing thinkers like Nietzsche and Foucault as public ironists, as critical both of the liberal democratic social and political formations that privatize autonomy, and of the slippery slope that allows the affirmation of the self's contingency to slide into a behaviouristic – and potentially barbaric (as in the case of psychiatry) – disciplining of the subject.

Second, although Rorty's liberalism does not presuppose the conception of the person *qua* possessive individual that one finds in classical liberal-ism, and although the liberal ironist has a Nietzschean awareness of herself as a tissue of contingencies, the Rortian ironical self is just as private as the possessive individual and its conception of liberty is just as negative.

Thus, although Rorty weakens the liberal conception of personhood, it does the same work as the possessive individual in underpinning liberalism, where freedom is defined negatively, that is to say, one is free in so far as one can distance oneself from social institutions.[8] Political freedom, for Rorty, is simply 'being left alone' (Rorty forthcoming, p. 17); or, more polemically, he writes, 'My private purposes . . . are none of your business' (Rorty 1989, p. 91). Against this negative conception of freedom, it is important to emphasize a positive conception of freedom, where liberty would not be found in the absence of normative constraint, but rather – the more Hegelian thought – that freedom would be precisely a product of such normative constraints (i.e. social practices), that is to say, freedom would be social and public and not a-social and private.[9]

Third, with regard to the public/private distinction; it seems strange that the fact that we become ironists in the private realm seems to have few implications for our relation to the public realm. It would appear that the public realm continues for 'we Rortians' in the same way as it did before we were transformed from metaphysicians into ironists. My question is a psychological one: namely, how can one be a Nietzschean ironist in the private sphere, which would mean understanding liberal principles of tolerance and abhorrence of cruelty as symptoms of *ressentiment*, and a liberal in the public sphere where one would respect and act on those principles? Does not the public/private distinction of the self into ironist and liberal yield an impossible psychological *bi-cameralism*, which would be a recipe for political cynicism (Nietzsche lurking behind a Millian mask)? To cite one of Rorty's own discussions, if one believes, with Freud, in the narcissistic origin of compassion, or that conscience is an ego-ideal for those unwilling to forgo the perfection of childhood (Rorty 1989, p. 31), then doesn't this alter one's practical, public relation to acts of compassion and the fact of conscience? The question of the psychological impossibility of being both a liberal and an ironist is compellingly raised in *Contingency, Irony and Solidarity* (Rorty 1989, p. 85), but is not convincingly dealt with in the ensuing discussion; Rorty raises the question extremely sharply and then proceeds to evade the issue. After having given no compelling reasons as to why a liberal should also be an ironist, Rorty goes on to claim, 'There is no reason the ironist cannot be a liberal.' This is true, but as it stands it still begs the psychological question of what it would feel like and what sort of psychological conflict would be produced by being a liberal ironist. Rorty just adds the caveat that an ironist 'Cannot be a "progressive" and "dynamic" liberal' (ibid., p. 91) and cannot display the same degree of social hope as the liberal metaphysician. But isn't this just to suggest that the liberal ironist is regressive, sedentary and hopeless – and what good is *that* sort of liberal?

Fourth, there is a large issue about Rorty's definition of the liberal: if a liberal is a person for whom cruelty is the worst thing that there is, then what is the status of the implied appeal to minimize cruelty? Is this a universal principle or foundation for moral obligation? If it is, then how would this be consistent with Rorty's anti-foundationalism, and if it is not, then what sort of binding power is it meant to have on members of liberal societies? Rorty goes on to qualify the abhorrence of cruelty by claiming that the recognition of a susceptibility to humiliation is the *only* social bond that is needed, and furthermore that this susceptibility to pain is pre-linguistic; suffering takes place outside of language (Rorty 1989, pp. 91, 94). To my mind, this would seem to ground Rorty's definition of the liberal in a universal fact about human nature. Thus, is not Rorty's definition of liberalism an attempt to ground the moral legitimacy of the political order in a claim about the pre-political state of nature, in a way that is strategically similar to Rousseau's appeal to *pitié* in the Second Discourse, which is defined as a pre-social, pre-rational sentient disposition that provokes compassion in the face of the other's suffering?[10] Are we not here being offered a redescription of a criterion for moral obligation grounded not in reason but in the response to suffering, a criterion which can also be found in Bentham's argument for the extension of moral obligations towards animals, 'The question is not, Can they Reason? nor Can they *talk*? but *Can they suffer*?'[11] Let me say that I do not disagree with either Rousseau or Bentham (or Rorty, if this is what he is claiming). I will argue below for a criterion of ethical obligation located in the sensible or sentient disposition of the self towards the other's suffering, which is to be found in the work of Emmanuel Levinas. It will be claimed that such a criterion for ethical obligation yields a concept of justice that is taken up by Derrida and which establishes the public significance of deconstruction. Of course, this will mean reading Levinas as more of a secular pragmatist (what Derrida would call an empiricist)[12] and less of a religious metaphysician. But – and this is the present point – is not this recognition of cruelty or suffering as the ethical basis for Rorty's liberalism an appeal to an essentialist, foundationalist fact about human nature; and does this not sit rather uneasily with the general drift of Rorty's intentions? Despite Rorty's claims to irony and the ubiquity of contingency, is he not in fact attempting to base moral obligation and political practice upon a foundational claim about human susceptibility to humiliation, upon a recognition of the other's suffering? And even if one were to relativize this claim and argue that only 'we liberals' recognize the avoidance of cruelty as the basis for morals and politics and that such recognition is a product of a particular – and therefore contingent – social and political history, does it not nevertheless remain true that the claim has the status of a non-relativizable universal for 'we liberals', with our set of 'we intentions'? Is cruelty something about which liberals can be ironic?[13]

Rorty's Reading of Derrida

Having sketched the general picture of Rorty's position in *Contingency, Irony and Solidarity*, it is possible to see how the pragmatist critique of philosophy so powerfully articulated in *Philosophy and the Mirror of Nature* extends into moral and political concerns to produce a purportedly anti-foundationalist reformulation of liberalism. In the remainder of this chapter I want to address two questions: how does Derrida's work fit into this picture, and is Rorty's picture of Derrida justified?

Rorty's concern with Derrida goes back to the late 1970s and in particular to an influential essay, 'Philosophy as a Kind of Writing' (Rorty 1982, pp. 90–109). In this essay, Rorty sees Derrida as an ally in his more general critique of Neo-Kantian analytic philosophy and representationalism. It is claimed that Derrida's work is best understood as the latest development in a non-Kantian tradition of dialectical thinking that begins with Hegel's *Phenomenology of Spirit*, where narrative is substituted for veridicality and world-disclosure for argument. Derrida recalls philosophy to its written status by the use of multi-lingual puns, allusions, typographical gimmicks, jokes and sexual innuendoes. In this way, Derrida shows that philosophy (with a lower case 'p' rather than Philosophy) is best described as a kind of writing or as a sector of culture devoted to the discussion of a particular tradition and not as the master discourse by which all other disciplines are to be judged. Deconstruction lets us imagine the way things might look if we did not have the Kantian representationalist model of Philosophy built into our culture. This theme is continued in the 1984 essay 'Deconstruction and Circumvention' (Rorty 1991b, pp. 85–106), where Rorty agrees with Habermas *avant la lettre* (and for quite un-Habermasian reasons), that deconstruction allows us to blur the distinction between philosophy and literature and to promote the idea of a 'seamless, undifferentiated general text' (Rorty 1991b, p. 85). In a nutshell, deconstruction does not engage us in an indeterminate task of deconstructing the tradition with the permanent risk of falling back within its limit, but rather allows us to *circumvent* the tradition, to go around it. Rorty claims that the Heidegger-inspired problematic of overcoming the tradition, or metaphysics, is a pseudo-problem that ought to be replaced by lots of little pragmatic questions.

Yet, from the very beginning of his encounter with deconstruction, Rorty inserts a note of caution with respect to both Derrida and, more particularly, Derrida's interpreters in the English-speaking world. For Rorty, Derrida's less interesting, less pragmatist side is revealed in his early work through his invocation of certain master-words like 'trace' and '*différance*'; words with a seemingly transcendental function in Derrida's discourse, which would risk deconstruction slipping back into the onto-theo-logical tradition it sought to undermine. Although Derrida, Rorty insists, always ultimately pulls back from this temptation to transcendent-alize, unconditionalize or divinize words like 'trace', and where Derrida is careful to point out that *différance* is not a metaphysical name,[14] the same caution is not shown by many of Derrida's interpreters.

Is Derrida a transcendental philosopher? Rorty raises this question in a 1989 essay which responds directly to the publication of Rodolphe Gasché's *The Tain of the Mirror* (Rorty 1991b, pp. 119–28). The appearance of Gasché's book allows Rorty to focus many of the objections he had to previous interpretations of Derrida, notably those of Jonathan Culler and Christopher Norris, each of which attempted to block Rorty's identi-fication of deconstruction with pragmatism by claiming that Derrida's work was full of rigorous arguments and had to be judged by traditional philosophical standards. Rorty's main problem with these interpreters is that they tend to treat Derrida as a quasi-metaphysician and not as an ironist; they want 'to make Derrida into a man with a great big theory about a great big subject' (Rorty forthcoming, p. 8) and they show the kind of reverence for philosophy that Rorty believes is ridiculed in a text like *La Carte postale*.

Everything turns here on the question of whether Derrida has argu-ments or not, that is to say, whether he can be admitted as a public thinker (and argumentation would be the criterion for admission) whose work has serious moral and political consequences. Gasché attempts to claim Derrida's work for serious philosophical consideration by showing that it forms what he calls 'a system beyond Being', that is to say, a series of infrastructures *(trace, différance, supplement, iterability, remark)* that are rigorously deduced from particular texts and which have a (quasi)-transcendental status, in so far as they make a claim to the conditions of possibility and impossibility for the particular text, or conceptual structure or institution under consideration.[15] Thus, Gasché's defence of Derrida as a rigorous philosopher turns on whether one can locate something akin to transcendental arguments in his work. If Derrida is a transcendental philosopher then, it is claimed, this will prevent deconstruction being caricatured as a mere private fantasy (although, for Rorty, to call Derrida a private fantasist is to pay him a much higher compliment than calling him a transcendental philosopher – Rorty 1991b, p. 121).

What, then, is an argument for Rorty? He follows Ernst Tugendhat (and, incidentally, the vast majority of philosophers in the European tradition) in claiming that argumentation has to be propositional, that is, argument can only be about the truth or meaning of propositions and therefore philosophical discourse must be propositional if it is properly to be called argumentative (Rorty 1991b, pp. 124–5).[16] There are only two directions one can follow on the basis of such a definition: either the language of argumentation (deductive or inductive) is antecedently given and stable, like the language of logic or what Rorty calls 'normal' science; or it is a disposable ladder-language of the kind employed by Wittgenstein in the *Tractatus*, a language that is to be left behind when *aufgehoben*. For Rorty, Derrida – like Wittgenstein and Hegel – is a master of *Aufhebung*. Thus, the claim that is central to Gasché's depiction of transcendental argumentation in Derrida, namely that one can move from the propositional to some pre-propositional level (i.e. *différance*) which would provide the conditions of possibility and impossibility for the propositional and, moreover, that one can claim some sort of cognitive status for such a procedure, is a *misunderstanding* of the nature of argumentation. For Rorty, argumentation requires that the same language be employed in one's premises and conclusions. Such a definition of argumentation would not disqualify traditional, Kantian forms of transcendental argument (which were concerned with resolving sceptical doubts about the existence of the self and the external world), but it does disqualify Derridean forms of (quasi)-transcendental argumentation which would attempt to locate the conditions of possibility and impossibility for propositional language in some pre-propositional 'word' or 'concept'. Thus, Gasché's attempt to claim Derrida for serious philosophical attention by arguing that he employs (quasi)-transcendental arguments is based on a misunderstanding of the nature of argumentation. Hence, Rorty concludes, Gasché's project collapses.[17]

For Rorty, deconstruction is not (quasi)-transcendental philosophy, but must be understood as part of a tradition of philosophy as world-disclosure, a tradition that includes Plato, Hegel and Heidegger, where our old vocabularies of self- and world-description are challenged, redescribed and replaced by new vocabularies. Thus, the crucial distinction to draw is that between an argumentative form of language which addresses the problems of social justice – what we called 'the public' – and a non-argumentative, often oracular, form of language that is world-disclosive and concerned with the quest for individual autonomy – what we called 'the private'. Failure to draw the distinction between the public and the private will lead, on the one hand, to the sort of reading that Carnap gives of Heidegger, and Habermas gives of Derrida, and, on the other hand, to the reading that Gasché gives of Derrida and – perhaps – that Derrida gives of Austin.

Rorty concludes 'Is Derrida a Transcendental Philosopher?' with the rhetorical question: should one read Derrida with Gasché as a transcendental latter-day Hegel, or with Rorty as a kind of French Wittgenstein (Rorty 1991b, p. 128)? Rorty adds that the response to this question is not straightforward because 'Derrida makes noises of both sorts' (Rorty 1989, p. 128). However, in order to persuade the reader to choose Rorty's interpretation over Gasché's, he offers what one might call a developmental thesis based on a distinction between Derrida's earlier and later work. Rorty divides Derrida's work into an earlier, professorial and scholarly period and a later eccentric, personal, original period. Derrida's early work, especially *De la grammatologie* is, for Rorty (and I think he is right) continuous with Heidegger's problematic of the overcoming of metaphysics and attempts to locate the conditions of possibility and impossibility for logocentrism in certain infrastructures, like 'trace' and '*différance*'. Thus, in his early work, Derrida is indeed deploying forms of (quasi)-transcendental argumentation and therefore Gasché's reading is valid for Derrida's early work (which also entails that Derrida himself was subject to the misunderstanding about the meaning of argumentation that Rorty raised against Gasché above). However, if Derrida's early work is engaged in a form of what Rorty calls 'ironist theorizing', then the crucial moment in Derrida's development occurs, for Rorty, in the move from grandiose theory to more minimal and private forms of writing.

This developmental thesis is intimated in the title of Rorty's discussion of Derrida in *Contingency, Irony and Solidarity: 'From* Ironist Theorizing *to* Private Allusions' (Rorty points out that he had originally wanted to entitle the discussion 'From Ironist Theorizing to Private *Jokes*' – Rorty 1991b, p. 120). For Rorty, the texts that best show this move from theory to privacy are *Glas* and, especially, *La Carte postale*; neither of which is discussed by Gasché in *The Tain of the Mirror*. Thus, for Rorty, Derrida's early theoretical work is a 'false start' in the same way, he claims, that *Sein und Zeit* is a false start in the development of Heidegger's work and the *Tractatus* was a false start for Wittgenstein. Rorty argues for 'the superiority of later to earlier Derrida' (Rorty 1991b, p. 124), and claims that this superiority lies in the move away from quasi-transcendental forms of theorizing and towards new forms of writing, that give expression to privacy, fantasy and humour. The later Derrida privatizes his philosophical thinking, drops theory and gives free rein to fantasy. In an intriguing formulation, Rorty writes that Derrida 'privatizes the sublime, having learnt from the fate of his predecessors [i.e. Heidegger] that the public can never be more than beautiful' (*Contingency, Irony and Solidarity,* p. 125). Thus, on this view, in a text like *La Carte postale*, Derrida does not resemble Heidegger so much as Proust, in so far as he is concerned less with the sublime ineffability of the word and more with the proliferation of beauty and the rearrangement of his memories. For Rorty, Derrida 'has done for the history of philosophy what Proust did for his life story': he has achieved autonomy through art. The consequence of this developmental thesis is that Derrida's work has no ethical, political or public significance in so far as it has given up on the attempt to reconcile theoretically the public and the private. It is this claim that I want to challenge.

Is Rorty's Reading of Derrida Justified?

I want to direct two questions to Rorty's reading of Derrida: first as to the validity of the developmental thesis, and second as to whether deconstruction can be said to have no public utility. Let me say, however, that I think Rorty's reading of Derrida, especially his interpretation of *La Carte postale* in *Contingency, Irony and Solidarity*, is an extremely strong reading that brings an honesty, humour and lightness of touch that are all too infrequent in discussions of Derrida, and which also offers a plausible approach to Derrida's more 'autobiographical' texts, like the recent *Circonfession*.[18] Also, and this is where I would part company with Gasché, I do not want to be drawn into a transcendental defence of Derrida against Rorty's pragmatized deconstruction. I think this strategy is too 'reactive' (in Nietzsche's sense), where a transcendental-philosophical defence of Derrida is itself a reaction to either a 'literary' assimilation of deconstruction (in the work of Geoffrey Hartman, Paul de Man and the Yale School) or to a Critical Theory-inspired critique of Derrida (in the work of Habermas or Manfred Frank). Also, it sets up an unhelpful opposition between the transcendental and the pragmatic, where philosophy becomes identified solely with the former against the latter.

As we saw above, much of the force of Rorty's understanding of deconstruction turns on his developmental account of Derrida's work. The question here is whether Derrida's early work is a false start and to what extent Rorty is justified in periodizing Derrida's work into early and late, particularly when the difference between early and late is only the matter of a few years or so and when Derrida is, to say the least, still going strong.[19] Can one really, with any plausibility, speak of a 'Derrida I' and a 'Derrida II', in the same way as William Richardson interpreted Heidegger (a distinction that Heidegger himself sought to complicate)?[20] On the contrary, I would claim that the difference between a text like *La Voix et le phénomène* and a text like *Glas* does not consist in any move from the public to the private, but rather suggests a change in the mode of presentation of Derrida's work, from a constative form of theorizing to a *performative* mode of writing, or, in other terms, from meta-language to language.[21] Unlike some (but by no means all) of Derrida's work from the 1960s, for example the opening chapters of *De la grammatologie*, much of his work in the 1970s is concerned less with formulating a theoretico-historico-interpretative grid (a 'science' of grammatology) and more with deconstruction(s) as a form of textual *enactment*, an event or series of events. Thus, the development of Derrida's work, if there is one, and this would have to be plotted in some detail (in my experience of reading Derrida, the closer one looks, the harder it is to find any substantial difference between earlier and later work; I am always astonished by the extraordinary thematic continuity of Derrida's work and the persistence of his central concerns), would not be found in any move from the public to the private, but from meta-language to language, from constative to performative utterance, allowing the performative constantly to overflow the constative.[22]

And yet, writing now, nearly twenty years after the publication of *Glas* and thirteen years after the publication of *La Carte postale*, there is also a large issue as to how one is to understand Derrida's more recent work, where the performative experiments of the 1970s have not been continued at such length (there are some examples, see Derrida [1987]) and where Derrida's work has, in my view, become dominated by the over-whelmingly *public* issue of *responsibility*, whether ethical, political, sexual, textual, legal or institutional. In order to address these issues, I would suggest – contentiously – that Derrida's style has become neither theoretical nor performative, but *quasi-phenomenological*. By this I mean that much of Derrida's recent work – his analyses of mourning, of the promise and the secret, of eating and sacrifice, of friendship and confession, of the gift and testimony – is concerned with the careful description and analysis of particular phenomena, in order to elucidate their deeply aporetic or undecidable structures. My contention here is that Derrida's work is moving towards a practice of deconstruction as a series of quasi-phenomenological micrologies that are concerned with the particular *qua* particular, that is to say, with the grain and enigmatic detail of everyday life.

This leads me to my second and more far-reaching question to Rorty's reading of Derrida, which arises as a consequence of his developmental thesis: namely, is it justified to claim that deconstruction has (or should have) no public significance, and can therefore have no ethical or political utility? In *The Ethics of Deconstruction: Derrida and Levinas*,[23] I argued that Derridian deconstruction can and indeed should be understood as an ethical demand, provided one understands ethics in the particular and novel sense given to that word in the work of Emmanuel Levinas. Crudely stated, ethics for Levinas is defined as the calling into question of my freedom and spontaneity, that is to say, my subjectivity, by the other person (*autrui*). Ethics is here conceived, in the wake of Buber's I–thou relation (although Levinas is ultimately critical of Buber), in terms of an ethical *relation* between persons. What distinguishes an ethical relation from other relations (to oneself or to objects) is, Levinas claims, that it is a relation with that which cannot be comprehended or subsumed under the categories of the understanding. In Stanley Cavell's terms, it is the very unknowability of the other, the irrefutability of scepticism, that initiates a relation to the other based on acknowledgement and respect.[24] The other person stands in a relation to me that exceeds my cognitive powers, placing me in question and calling me to justify myself. Levinas's philosophical ambition is to subordinate claims to knowledge to claims to justice, or, in Kantian terms, to establish the primacy of practical reason (although, for Levinas, the ethical is the pre-rational foundation of the rational rather than the exemplification of reason). As Levinas is often given to write, *ethics is first philosophy*.

Although severely critical of Heidegger's philosophy after *Sein und Zeit*

and his political myopia, Levinas shares his early critique of the theor-
eticism or intellectualism of Husserlian intentionality, where, it is claimed,
the subject maintains an objectifying relation to the world mediated
through representation: the worldly object is the *noema* of a *noesis*. Levinas
follows Heidegger's ontological undermining of the theoretical comport-
ment towards the world (*Vorhandenheit*) and of the subject/object distinction that supports epistemology, by tracing intentionality back to a
more fundamental stratum, namely, sentience or sensibility. Simply stated,
Levinas shows how intentional consciousness is conditioned by *life*, by the
material conditions of existence. His work offers, I believe, *a material
phenomenology of subjective life*, where the conscious subject of representation and intentionality is reduced to the sentient subject of sensibility.
Levinas's phenomenological claim – and by 'phenomenology' Levinas
means a methodological adherence to the spirit rather than the letter of
Husserlian intentional analysis, that is to say, the description of the
constitutive structures of naïve conscious life – is that the deep structure
of subjective experience is always already engaged in a relation of
responsibility or, better, responsivity to the other. The ethical relation takes
place at the level of sensibility, not at the level of consciousness, and thus,
in a way that recalls both Bentham's and Rousseau's criteria for ethical
obligation mentioned above, it is in my pre-reflective sentient disposition
towards the other's suffering that a basis for ethics and responsibility can
be found.[25]

What is the relation of this Levinasian account of ethics to the debate
between Derrida and Rorty? First, with regard to Rorty, although he
would doubtless criticize Levinas's claim that ethics is first philosophy as
a Neo-Kantian philosophical foundationalism, and although Levinas's
qualified endorsement of Husserlian phenomenological method would sit
rather uneasily with Rorty's pragmatism, there is room to ask how far
apart Rorty and Levinas really are from each other. Are not Rorty's
definition of liberalism and Levinas's definition of ethics essentially doing
the same work, that is, attempting to locate a source for moral and political
obligation in a sentient disposition towards the other's suffering? Do they
both not agree that cruelty is the worst thing that there is, and that,
furthermore, this is the only social bond that we need?

Second, with regard to Derrida, I would like to make good a *rapproche-
ment* between Levinas and Derrida by looking at one recent example from
Derrida's work. My argument here can be more formally stated along the
following lines: first, let us recall that Rorty defines the private as being
concerned with 'idiosyncratic projects of self-overcoming', whereas the
public is defined as 'having to do with the suffering of other human
beings'. If I can make good the claim that deconstruction is ethical in the
peculiarly Levinasian sense identified above, then deconstruction would
be concerned with the suffering of other human beings and would

therefore qualify as public by Rorty's own criteria. Deconstruction could then have significant ethical and political consequences. If Rorty is a liberal, then, I would claim, Levinas and Derrida are also liberals – which perhaps begs the question as to the adequacy of Rorty's definition of liberalism.

The example I have in mind is the first half of Derrida's remarkable text on the question of justice, 'Force of Law: The "Mystical Foundation of Authority"'.[26] Derrida makes some remarkably provocative statements in this text; he writes, 'Justice in itself, if such a thing exists, outside or beyond law, is not deconstructible. No more than deconstruction itself, if such a thing exists. Deconstruction is justice' (Derrida 1992, pp. 14–15). Derrida's discussion proceeds from the distinction between law, which is deconstructable, and which, it is claimed, *must* be deconstructable if political progress is to be possible, and justice, which is not deconstructable, but is that in virtue of which deconstruction takes place. In a quasi-transcendental register, Derrida claims that justice is the undeconstructable condition of possibility for deconstruction, that 'nothing is more just than what I today call deconstruction' (ibid., p. 21). On the basis of references to Montaigne and Pascal (and even a rare allusion to Wittgenstein on p. 14), Derrida paradoxically defines justice as an experience of that which we are not able to experience, which is qualified as 'the mystical', 'the impossible' or 'aporia'. In Derrida's more habitual vocabulary, justice is an 'experience' of the undecidable. However, and this is crucial, such an undecidable experience of justice does not arise in some intellectual intuition or theoretical deduction, rather it always arises in relation to a particular entity, to the singularity of the other (ibid., p. 20). It is at this point (or, to be precise, at two points: pp. 22, 27) in the discussion that Derrida cites Levinas and employs the latter's conception of justice to illuminate his own account. In *Totality and Infinity*,[27] justice defines and is defined by the ethical relation to the other, '*la relation avec autrui – c'est à dire la justice*' (p. 22); that is to say, justice arises in the particular and non-subsumptive relation to the other, as a response to suffering that demands an infinite responsibility. Thus it can be seen that when Derrida is provoked into offering an illustration of the public significance of deconstruction by showing how it presupposes a conception of justice, he draws heavily from Levinas.

This allusion to Levinas seems unproblematic until one realizes that there are *two* conceptions of justice in Levinas. As Levinas points out in the 1987 Preface to the German translation of *Totalité et infini*, justice functions as a synonym for the ethical in the latter work, in just the way discussed by Derrida.[28] However, in Levinas's later work, particularly *Autrement qu'être ou au-delà de l'essence*,[29] justice is distinguished from the ethical relation, where Levinas argues that the question of justice arises when a third party arrives on the scene, obliging one to choose between competing ethical claims and reminding one that the ethical relation is always already situated in a specific socio-political context.[30] The fact that Derrida adopts an *ethical* and not a *political* concept of justice from Levinas does not mean, however, that the deconstructive account of justice is a-political. Derrida claims that it is linked to what he calls '*politicization*' (Levinas 1974, p. 28), and as examples of this process he cites the Declaration of the Rights of Man and the abolition of slavery, that is to say, the emancipatory gains of classical liberalism. In a staggeringly blunt statement, Derrida writes, 'Nothing seems to me less outdated than the classical emancipatory ideal' (although we might want to ask: is Derrida's commitment to this emancipatory ideal necessarily a commitment to liberalism, or might it not entail a more radical version of this ideal that one can find, for example, in the socialist tradition?). Thus, the ethical conception of justice that drives the deconstructive enterprise and which is defined in terms of responsibility to the other would (Derrida, characteristically, adds 'perhaps' – p. 27) seem to be essentially connected to the possibility of political reformation, transformation and progress, opening up a future of political possibilities.

To summarize, Derrida's claim here is that deconstruction is justice and justice is an 'experience' of the undecidable; that is to say, according to my interpretation, to be just is to recognize one's infinite responsibility before the singular other as something over which one cannot ultimately decide, as something that exceeds my cognitive powers. It is this 'experience' of justice that propels one forward into politics, that is to say, from undecidability to the decision, to what Derrida calls, following Kierkegaard, the madness of the decision (ibid., p. 26).[31] Politics is the realm of the decision, of the organization and administration of the public realm, of the institution of law and policy. As I see it, the central aporia of deconstruction – an aporia that must not be avoided if any responsible political activity is to be undertaken – concerns the nature of this passage from undecidability to the decision, from the ethical 'experience' of justice to political action, to what we might call the moment of judgement. But how does this deconstructive, ethical conception of justice translate into political judgement? Derrida insists that judgements have to be made and decisions have to be taken, provided it is understood that to be responsible they must pass through an experience of the undecidable. But my *critical* question to Derrida would be: *what* decisions are taken, *which* judgements are made?[32]

For Derrida, no political form can or should attempt to embody justice, and the undecidability of justice must always lie outside the public realm, guiding, criticizing and deconstructing that realm, but never being instantiated within it. From a deconstructive perspective, the greatest danger in politics is the threat of totalitarianism, or what Jean-Luc Nancy calls 'immanentism',[33] in all of its most recent and terrifying disguises: neo-fascism, nationalism, ethnocentrism, theocracy. Totalitarianism is premised upon the identification of the political and the social and would claim that a particular political form and hence a particular state, community or territory embodies justice, that justice is immanent to the body politic. A deconstructive approach to politics, based upon the radical separation of justice from law, and the non-instantiability of the former within the latter, leads to what one might call the dis-embodiment of justice, where no state, community or territory could be said to embody justice. One might say that the 'experience' of justice is that of an absolute alterity or transcendence that guides politics without being fully present in the public realm. If we look back to Derrida's first published work on Husserl, we might say that justice is an 'Idea in the Kantian sense', an infinitely deferred ethico-teleological postulate that continually escapes the horizon of presence and the very idea of a horizon.[34]

If it is now asked what political form best maintains this dis-embodiment of justice, then I take it that Derrida's response would be *democracy*: not a democracy that claims to instantiate justice here and now, not an apolegetics for actually existing liberal democracy (but neither a dismissal of the latter), but a democracy guided by the *futural* or *projective* transcendence of justice – what Derrida calls *une démocratie à venir*.[35] To my mind, this would seem to commit Derrida to a utopian and critical politics that does not differ substantially from the Deweyan tradition that seeks to link pragmatism to radical democracy – the very political tradition in whose lineage Rorty claims to stand. However, if my argument is not entirely aberrant, if Rorty and Derrida share similar public and political aspirations (even though they are quite differently articulated), then why is Rorty unable to see in Derrida a powerful political ally?

Conclusion

I hope to have shown that Derrida both conceives of himself as a public thinker, whose work has serious ethical commitments and political consequences, and that he can only be so understood on the basis of Rorty's own criteria for distinguishing the public from the private and liberalism from irony. The undeconstructable condition of possibility for deconstruction is a commitment to justice, defined in terms of an ethical relation to the other, a response to suffering that provokes an infinite responsibility and the attempt to minimize cruelty. Such an ethical conception of justice can never be fully instantiated in the public realm, nor can it be divorced from the latter; rather justice regulates public space, making politics critical, utopian and radically democratic.

In terms of the theme of this discussion, deconstruction and pragmatism, it has hopefully been established that Rorty's picture of Derrida as only a private ironist falls rather short of the truth. Although, as I admitted at the outset, it might be valid to interpret concepts like '*différance*' in terms of a pragmatist notion of context, thereby showing the contingency of language, self and world, it is by now hopefully clear that what motivates the practice of deconstruction is an ethical conception of justice, that is, by Rorty's criteria, public and liberal. Thus, deconstruction is pragmatist, *but it is not pragmatist all the way down*. At the basis of deconstruction is a non-pragmatist (or at least non-Rortian) foundational commitment to justice as something that cannot be relativized, or at least cannot be relativized for 'we liberals'. Of course, the consequence of my conclusion is that Derrida is still seeking to fulfil the classical philosophical project of reconciling the public and the private, believed by Rorty to be redundant. If deconstruction is justice, then this commitment to justice *goes all the way down*: in private self-creation as well as public responsibility.

However, the intriguing counter-balancing question that this essay has thrown up is whether Rorty's pragmatism is in fact pragmatist *all the way down*; or whether its commitment to liberalism – in terms of a non-relativizable claim about the susceptibility of human beings to suffering and the need to minimize cruelty – transgresses the limits of Rorty's pragmatism. Can pragmatism maintain a genuine and non-cynical commitment to liberalism and still remain pragmatist *all the way down*?

Notes

1 Might not Derrida also ironize about Rorty's conception of the history of philosophy, what Rorty calls 'the Plato–Kant succession': a vision of the history of philosophy that is just as totalizing, unilateral and univocal as Heidegger's, and which reads irony out of the pre-Kantian tradition (but what about Socrates? And can we always take Descartes at his word?). From what vantage point does Rorty view history? If history is a series of successive metaphors and displaced final vocabularies, a history whose metaphoricity is now grasped fully for the first time, then it must be asked, from where and from what final vocabulary do we view that history? Is Rorty's not a God's eye-view on the impossibility of any God's eye-view?

2 With regard to Rorty's earlier work, particularly *Philosophy and the Mirror of Nature*, let me a venture a couple of professions of mixed faith: first, I agree with Rorty's critique of the mind as the mirror of nature and hence with his critique of representationalism, epistemology and hence philosophy itself, if the latter is conceived in narrowly epistemological terms. My only caveat here is that I would arrive at the same conclusion as Rorty through Heidegger's critique of epistemology and Neo-Kantianism in *Sein und Zeit*. In my view, however, this would still leave open the possibility of a form of philosophizing, exemplified in the phenomenology of the early Heidegger, the later Merleau-Ponty and Levinas, that would be critical of the slide in Rorty's work from the critique of epistemology into naturalism (on this point, see Bernstein [1992]). Second, I am very sympathetic to Rorty's attempted de-divinization of the world, where a Davidsonian account of language, a Nietzschean/Freudian account of the self and culture, and a Darwinian account of nature all conspire to produce a relation to the world conceived as a web or tissue of contingencies. Yet, it seems to me that the outcome of the recognition of contingency might

not be a move towards naturalism, but rather towards *romanticism*, namely the romantic victory of poetry over philosophy announced in *Contingency, Irony and Solidarity* (Rorty 1989, p. 40), where the triumph of metaphor and self-creation over literalness and discovery leads to a romantic demand for a poeticization of the world, a re-enchantment of the world as a web of contingencies.

3 See Macpherson (1966), esp. pp. 1–11.
4 Putnam (1992), p. 199.
5 Ball, T. *et al.* (1990), pp. 118–20.
6 Ibid., pp. 104–8.
7 See Virilio (1991) and Shapiro (1993).
8 For a related line of criticism, with reference to Rorty's conception of autonomy, see Caputo (1993), esp. pp. 165–6.
9 This view is argued for in Brandom (1979). In this connection, see Rorty's discussion of Brandom in 'Representation, Social Practice and Truth' in Rorty (1991a), pp. 151–61.
10 Rousseau, *Discours sur l'origine de l'inégalité parmi les hommes*, Paris, Garnier, p. 37.
11 Bentham, *An Introduction to the Principles of Morals and Legislation*, eds J.H. Burns and H.L.A. Hart, London, Athlone, 1970, p. 283.
12 See 'Violence et métaphysique', in Derrida (1967), p. 224.
13 A similar line of argument is proposed with respect to Rorty in Wolf (1993), see esp. p. 63–4.
14 Rorty repeatedly cites sentences from the closing paragraphs of Derrida's 1968 paper 'La différance' (in Derrida 1972a, pp. 28–9), where he claims that there is no unique name or name for Being, and that this must be thought without Heideggerian nostalgia or hope (see Rorty 1982, p. 103; 1989, p. 122; 1991b, p. 95).
15 See Gasché (1986).
16 See Tugendhat (1979). For example, Tugendhat writes, '*alles intentionale Bewusstsein überhaupt ist propositional*' (p. 20).
17 For Gasché's critique of Tugendhat's position, where he argues that to restrict oneself to propositional truth is to deprive oneself of the possibility of thinking the foundations of the propositional, see Gasché (1986) pp. 76–7.
18 In Bennington and Derrida (1991).
19 It would not be difficult, on the basis of textual evidence, to make the distinction between earlier and later Derrida begin to look absurd. For example, I take it that most of the essays from *Marges* (1972) would be judged by Rorty to belong to the style of the early Derrida, whilst portions of *Dissémination* (also, 1972) and *Glas* (only two years later in 1974) would be classified as later Derrida.
20 See Heidegger's *Vorwort* to Richardson (1963), pp. xxii–xxiii.
21 I owe this thought to conversations with Gasché.
22 Of course, this transition from meta-language to language may well prove to be impossible; but, as I have tried to show elsewhere (Critchley [1988]), it is this very impossibility that is being explored in *Glas*. In this connection, see Geoffrey Bennington's extremely insightful discussion in Bennington and Derrida (1991).
23 See Critchley (1992), Ch.1, pp. 1–58.
24 See 'Scepticism and the Problem of Others' in Cavell (1979), pp. 327–496.
25 See Levinas (1984).
26 See Derrida (1992), pp. 3–67. All subsequent page references inserted into the text.
27 Levinas (1990).

28 Ibid., p. II.
29 Levinas (1974).
30 Ibid., pp. 199–207.
31 A quote which also provided the epigraph to Derrida's celebrated essay on Foucault, see Derrida (1967), p. 51.
32 Such a question opens the large and difficult issue of specifying the precise relation between undecidability and the decision, justice and judgement, and ethics and politics in Derrida's work; which is, to say the least, a problem of which he is acutely aware, and which might be said to dominate much of his recent work. In this connection, see Critchley (1992), pp. 188–247; Laclau and Mouffe (1985) and Laclau (1990), where the problem of the relation of deconstruction and politics is theorized in terms of an expanded concept of hegemony.
33 See Nancy (1990).
34 See Derrida (1962).
35 See Derrida (1991).

References

Ball, T. *et al* (1990), 'Review Symposium on Richard Rorty', *History of the Human Sciences*, vol. 3, no. 1, pp. 101–22.

Bennington, G. and Derrida, J. (1991), *Jacques Derrida*. Paris, Seuil.

Bentham, J. (1970), *An Introduction to the Principles of Morals and Legislation*, London, Athlone.

Bernstein, J. (1992), 'De-Divinization and the Vindication of Everyday Life: Reply to Rorty', *Tijdschrift voor Filosofie*, vol. 54, no. 4, pp. 668–92.

Brandom, R. (1979), 'Freedom and Constraint by Norms', *American Philosophical Quarterly*, vol. 16, no. 3, pp. 187–96.

Caputo, J.D. (1993), 'On Not Circumventing the Quasi-Transcendental: The Case of Rorty and Derrida', in G. Madison (ed.), *Working Through Derrida*, Evanston, Northwestern University Press.

Cavell, S. (1979), *The Claim of Reason*, New York, Oxford University Press.

Critchley, S.J. (1988), 'A Commentary on Derrida's Reading of Hegel in *Glas*', *Bulletin of the Hegel Society of Great Britain*, no. 18, pp. 6–32.

Critchley, S.J. (1992), *The Ethics of Deconstruction*, Oxford, Blackwell.

Derrida, J. (1962), Introduction to *L'Origine de la géométrie*, Paris, Presses Universitaires de France.

Derrida, J. (1967), *L'Écriture et la différence*, Paris, Minuit.

Derrida, J. (1972a), *Marges de la philosophie*, Paris, Minuit.

Derrida, J. (1972b), *Dissémination*, Paris, Seuil.

Derrida, J. (1974), *Glas*, Paris, Galilée.

Derrida, J. (1987), *Feu la cendre*, Paris, Editions des femmes.

Derrida, J. (1991), *L'Autre cap*, Paris, Minuit.

Derrida, J. (1992), 'Force of Law: The "Mystical Foundation of Authority"', in D. Cornell, M. Rosenfeld and D.G. Carlson (eds), *Deconstruction and the Possibility of Justice*, London and New York, Routledge.

Gasché, R. (1986), *The Tain of the Mirror. Derrida and the Philosophy of Reflection*, Cambridge, Mass., Harvard University Press.

Laclau, E. (1990), *New Reflections on the Revolution of Our Time*, London, Verso.

Laclau, E. and Mouffe, C. (1985), *Hegemony and Socialist Strategy*, London, Verso.

Levinas, E. (1974), *Autrement qu'être ou au-delà de l'essence*, The Hague, Martinus Nijhoff.

40 Simon Critchley

Levinas, E. (1984), 'La Souffrance inutile', in *Cahiers de la nuit surveillée*, no. 3, pp. 329–38.
Levinas, E. (1990), *Totalité et Infini*, Paris, Livre de Poche.
Macpherson, C.B. (1966), *The Real World of Democracy*, New York, Oxford University Press.
Nancy, J.-L., (1990), *La Communauté désœuvrée*, Paris, Christian Bourgois.
Putnam, H. (1992), *Renewing Philosophy*, Cambridge, Mass., Harvard University Press.
Richardson, W.J. (1963), *Through Phenomenology to Thought*, The Hague, Martinus Nijhoff.
Rorty, R. (1980), *Philosophy and the Mirror of Nature*, Princeton, NJ, Princeton University Press.
Rorty, R. (1982), *The Consequences of Pragmatism*, Minnesota, University of Minnesota Press.
Rorty, R. (1989), *Contingency, Irony and Solidarity*, Cambridge, Cambridge University Press.
Rorty, R. (1991a), *Objectivism, Relativism and Truth. Philosophical Papers Volume 1*, Cambridge, Cambridge University Press.
Rorty, R. (1991b), *Essays on Heidegger and Others. Philosophical Papers Volume 2*, Cambridge, Cambridge University Press.
Rorty, R. (forthcoming), 'Habermas, Derrida and the Functions of Philosophy', *Revue Internationale de Philosophie*. All references to an unpublished typescript.
Rousseau, J.J. (1962), *Discours sur l'origine de l'inégalité parmi les hommes*, Paris, Garnier.
Shapiro, M.J. (1993), 'That Obscure Object of Violence: Logistics and Desire in the Gulf War', in D. Campbell and M. Dillon (eds) *The Political Subject of Violence*, Manchester, Manchester University Press.
Tugendhat, E. (1979), *Selbstbewusstsein und Selbstbestimmung*, Frankfurt an Main, Suhrkamp.
Virilio, P. (1991), *L'Écran du désert*, Paris, Galilée.
Wolf, U. (1993), 'Moral Controversies and Moral Theory', *European Journal of Philosophy*, vol. 1, no. 1, pp. 58–68.

4

Response to Simon Critchley

Richard Rorty

I agree with Simon Critchley that I have, in the past, made too much of the difference between earlier and later Derrida, and that 'the closer one looks, the harder it is to find any substantial difference between earlier and later work'. The more one reads either Heidegger or Derrida, the more continuities between the earlier and the later writings appear. But I should still claim that just as all that programmatic throat-clearing stuff about 'phenomenological ontology' at the beginning of *Being and Time* was something which Heidegger would have done better to have edited out, so all that supposedly deep stuff about the primordiality of the trace in Derrida's earlier work looks like a young philosophy professor, still a bit unsure of himself, making quasi-professional noises.

I also agree with Critchley that if 'one understands ethics in the particular and radical sense given to that word' by Levinas, then Derrida's practice may well have 'an overriding ethical significance'. But I don't understand the word 'ethics' that way, and I don't think that it useful to give that word that sense.

I don't find Levinas's Other any more useful than Heidegger's Being – both strike me as gawky, awkward, and unenlightening. I see ethics as what we have to start creating when we face a choice between two irreconcilable actions, each of which would, in other circumstances, have been equally natural and proper. Neither my child nor my country is very much like a Levinasian Other, but when I face a choice between incriminating my child or breaking my country's laws by committing perjury, I start looking around for some ethical principles. I may not find any that help, but that is another question. My failure to do so is not satisfactorily explained by reference to an Abyss that separates me from an Other.

Again, though Critchley has textual warrant for attributing this view to Derrida, I do not see that, as he puts it, 'Deconstruction is justice, and justice is an experience of the unexperiencable'. I do not see the point of defining a commonly used term such as 'justice' as the name of an impossibility. Granted that there are limit situations in which neither familiar practice nor familiar language offers anything very useful, it is no help to characterize what is going on in such situations as a self-contradiction. I think of justice as muddling through – in the way judges do when deciding hard cases, and parents do when trying to figure out whether to inform the police about what their children are up to. It seems to me pointless hype to dramatize our difficulties in knowing what to do by labelling our goal 'indescribable', 'unexperiencable', 'unintelligible', or 'infinitely distant'.

Unlike Critchley, I don't think we need a 'supreme ethical principle', any more than we need to ask whether we have a pre-reflective and pre-sentient set of responses to others' pains. I do not see the point of delving down to the roots of the difference between people who care about others' suffering and those who don't. For all I know, the difference is all acculturation, or all a matter of the environment of the first few days of infancy, or all in the genes. Maybe it's acculturation in some people and genes in others. I don't see why this should matter.

Levinas and Critchley are not in the same line of business as Dewey and I. I am not, as Critchley thinks I might be and probably should be, trying to 'locate a source of moral obligation in the sentient disposition of the self towards the Other's suffering', nor in any other sort of 'universal fact of human nature'. Maybe there is such a sentient disposition, but it is so malleable – so capable of being combined with indifference to the suffering of people of the wrong sorts – that it gives us precious little to rely on. We should just thank our lucky stars that there are quite a lot of people nowadays who are pretty consistently appalled by human beings suffering unnecessarily.

With luck – and especially with affluence and security[1] – there will be more and more such people. Some of them will be liberal ironists like Nabokov, Bloom and Derrida himself (examples who seem to me sufficient to rebut Critchley's doubts that it is psychologically possible to be both a liberal and an ironist). Some of them will be unimaginative, literal-minded, unromantic, decent dullards. We can use as many of both kinds of people as we can get.

Critchley suggests that naturalism doesn't go well with romanticism, and that the fruit of the recognition of contingency should be the latter but not the former. I see no tension between the two. Even if I were convinced by Freud's account of the narcissistic origin of compassion (which Critchley cites as an appropriate object of my concern), I would see no reason to become less romantic, less liberal, or less ironic. (Nor, I think, would Wordsworth or Emerson, had they been able to read Freud.) If natural science eventually tells me that compassion, like heterosexuality, can be eliminated by fiddling with a chromosome, I am not likely to change any of my attitudes or any of my behaviour. I see the Enlightenment as having cleared the way for both naturalism (in the sense of an account of human beings which makes the only big difference between them and giraffes the ability to use language) and romanticism (in the sense of exultation in human beings' ability to use language in new, suprising, ecstatic ways).

I hesitate to lug out the ultimate weapon so soon, but Critchley's attitudes strike me as – yes, you guessed it – *metaphysical*. I take pragmatists and deconstructionists to be united in thinking that anything can be anything if you put in the right context, and that 'right' just means the context that best serves somebody's purposes at a certain time and place. Metaphysicians think that there is a Right Context, where things are seen as they truly are, without reference to anybody's purposes. So they look for ultimate sources of this, and indefeasible presuppositions of that. Critchley keeps suggesting that moral seriousness requires us to conduct such a search. I think that if you can manage to act decently you can take moral seriousness or leave it alone. That is another reason why I see no problem about the psychological possibility of liberal ironism.

Critchley's endorsement, in a footnote, of Gasché's criticism of Tugendhat seems to me betray his penchant (shared with Gasché) for metaphysics. I thought that criticism the least persuasive part of Gasché's book. As I see it, if we could ever stop trying to get beneath the propositional to the non-propositional, we should have pretty well over-come the metaphysician's need for getting behind Appearance to Reality. For the nice thing about propositions is that they cry out for context, and they don't mind changing their message depending upon their surround-ings. They are the paradigm case of the perpetually relativizable and recontextualizable. The bad thing about the philosophers' candidates for the non-propositional basis of the propositional is that these candidates sit there smugly (like Austin's frog at the bottom of the beer-mug), thinking that they don't have and don't need a context.

I think it was the beginning of wisdom in philosophy of language when Frege said that words only have meaning in the context of a sentence. Quine, Derrida and Davidson have carried through on Frege's con-textualism – Quine in his claim that a sentence has meaning only in the context of a lot of other sentences, Derrida in his suggestion that the Book give place to the text, and Davidson in his pregnant remark that 'There is no such thing as a language.' Tugendhat supplements these philosophers by carrying through on Wittgenstein's suggestion that we change the subject of philosophy of language from meaning to use.[2]

There is a connection between my claim that naturalism and romanti-cism are not only compatible, but natural allies, and my anxiety to defend Tugendhat against Gasché. It is important for me to maintain that, although naturalism can explain how a certain species of animals could come to develop cooperative projects of exchanging marks and noises, and thus can explain the origin of language, it does so precisely by eschewing reference to anything that is both non-propositional and philosophically interesting (like Platonic Forms, or ideas in the mind of God, or *trace*, or *différance*). We naturalists insist that no transcendental conditions of possibility need be found for language – nor, *a fortiori*, for any other human activity. Banal causal conditions of actuality are enough. We can get our romantic kicks out of freshly minted, or freshly recontextualized, propositions, without thinking that these propositions may get us closer to something that lies beyond time, space, causality and chance.

One difference between Derrideans like Critchley and Deweyans like myself is that Derrida likes to put things in question, whereas Dewey insisted on asking 'What's the problem?' Our attitude is: if it isn't broken, don't fix it. Keep on using it until you can think of some other sort of tool which might do the job better. Derrideans tend to think that the more questioning, problematizing and *mettant-en-abîme* you can squeeze into the day's work, the better. Deweyans, on the other hand, think that you should only question when you find yourself in what Dewey called a 'problematic situation' – a situation in which you are no longer sure of what you are doing. You may not be sure what you want, or you may not be sure that your old tools are the best ways of getting what you want, or your perplexity may involve both kinds of uncertainty at once. But unless you suffer from some such uncertainty, you should save problematizing for weekends.

This does not mean that watching somebody else put something in question, for purposes of his or her own, may not awaken – accidentally, so to speak – an uncertainty in your own breast about one or another of your own projects. Both Proust and Derrida sometimes produce such uncertainty. Critchley is right in saying that, on my reading, Derrida resembles Proust more than he does Nietzsche or Heidegger, but I would not say, as he suggests I do, that 'Derrida's work has no ethical, political or public significance', any more than I would say this about Proust. Reading Proust sometimes makes a considerable difference to lots of people's subsequent descriptions of themselves and their projects. Reading Derrida sometimes has the same effect. On my non-Levinasian, Deweyan, notion of ethics, you can, *per accidens*, get a lot of ethical uncertainty, and sometimes even a little ethical guidance, out of the work of both.

Still, Critchley is quite right in saying that I would not assign much *political* significance to either Proust or Derrida. I agree with Richard Bernstein that to understand Derrida's motives one most see his work against a political background – and in particular against the background of the Holocaust. But I also agree with Thomas McCarthy that deconstruction is marginal to politics – that if you want to do some political work, deconstructing texts is not a very efficient way to set about it. Getting rid of phallogocentrism, metaphysics and all that is an admirable long-term cultural goal, but there is still a difference between such goals and the relatively short-term goals served by political deliberation and decision.

In the United States there are, alas, a large number of admirers of Derrida who see writing in his manner as their contribution to the relief of human suffering and the enlargement of human freedom. This Derridean left acquired a bad reputation, because it was invidiously contrasted with the sort of left that organizes strikes, lobbies legislators, puts forward candidates for Congress, writes newspaper editorials, and the like. I have made a lot of such invidious contrasts myself.[3] The main reason I make them is that I see politics, at least in democratic countries, as something to be conducted in as plain, blunt, public, easy-to-handle language as possible. I see the enemies of human happiness as just greed, sloth and hypocrisy, and I don't see the need for philosophical depth charges in dealing with such surface enemies.

Critchley is largely right in saying that I 'refuse the rich critical potential of seeing writers like Nietzsche and Foucault as public ironists'. I think that cartoonists like Trudeau and Herblock in the US, and various contributors to Le Canard Enchaîné in France, have a lot more critical potential as public ironists – as purveyors of fruitful redescriptions of the behaviour of our leaders – than do philosophers. It is true that Foucault, unlike Nietzsche, did offer some sensible political advice: he explained what to watch out for when dealing with psychiatrists, social workers, professors of various social sciences, and the like. Nevertheless, when public irony is what is wanted, philosophers and social theorists (except for the occasional Veblen) are usually not the best people to turn to.

A traditional difference between European and American intellectuals has been that the latter think that the moral and political decisions we face as individuals and as citizens are pretty clear, and that the vocabulary in which we typically formulate them does not need extensive revision. So they are slow to recognize the relevance of philosophy to politics, and inclined to think of philosophy as something you can take or leave alone – something which need not be approached in a spirit of moral seriousness. The Derridean left in the US has tried to make the Americans more European in this respect. I hope it fails in this attempt, because I think that in this respect at least, we Americans have bettered the instruction.

So, in the end, the big difference between Critchley and myself may be straightforwardly political rather than philosophical. As I see contemporary politics, we do not need what Critchley calls 'a critique of liberal society'. We just need more liberal societies, and more liberal laws in force within each such society. I see European philosophical thought as still dominated by the Marxist notion of Ideologiekritik, and by the romantic notion of the philosopher as the person who penetrates behind the appearances of present social institutions to their reality. I distrust both notions.

My principal reason for distrusting them is a political guess about which are the most efficient causal mechanisms for fruitful institutional change. My suspicion of metaphysics, and of the whole contrast between Appearance and Reality, is, politically speaking, just an optional extra. As somebody trained in philosophy, I get most of my romantic kicks out of metaphysics-bashing. As a citizen of a democratic state, I do not think that metaphysics-bashing is – except in the very long term – of much use.[4]

Notes

1 I say more about this in my 'Human Rights, Rationality and Sentimentality' in *On Human Rights: The 1993 Oxford Amnesty Lectures*, eds Susan Hurley and Stephen Shute, New York, Basic Books, 1993, pp. 112–34.
2 That is very different from doing what Critchley describes Wittgenstein as doing – *reducing* meaning to use. Metaphysicians reduce things to other things. Pragmatists and deconstructionists are forbidden to reduce – for that would mean that they had boiled down Appearance to its constituent Reality.
3 See my 'Movements and Campaigns,' *Dissent* (Winter, 1995) and my 'Two Cheers for the Cultural Left', *South Atlantic Quarterly* no. 89 (1990), pp. 227–34.
4 For some discussion of the possible long-term social benefits of metaphysics-bashing, as opposed to any short-term influence on institutions, see the closing sections of my 'Does Academic Freedom Have Philosophical Presuppositions?', *Academe* 80, no. 6 (November/December 1994), pp. 52–63.

5

Deconstruction, Pragmatism, Hegemony

Ernesto Laclau

I am writing here as a political theorist rather than as a philosopher in the strict sense of the term. My main purpose is to show how and why the two currents of thought whose comparison is the main aim of this book, are relevant for central aspects of a contemporary theorization of politics. This relevance can be shown, I think, in connection with a whole range of issues which have acquired an increasing significance both in advanced industrial societies and Third World countries. I have sustained in my own work that 'hegemony' is the central category for a theorization of politics.[1] The reasons for this claim will become clear, I hope, in the course of this essay. I will approach this issue, however, in an indirect way, through a discussion of both 'deconstruction' and 'pragmatism' which will attempt to show how the radicalization of both approaches requires, at some point in their respective arguments, that they are continued in terms very close to what I would call a 'logic' of hegemony.

Let's start with deconstruction. A deconstructive approach is highly relevant to two dimensions of the political – as opposed to the 'social' – which have acquired an increasing centrality in current debates. The first is the notion of the political as the *instituting* moment of society. The dominant vision of the political in the nineteenth century, prolonged into the twentieth by various sociologistic tendencies, had made of it a 'subsystem' or 'superstructure', submitted to the necessary laws of society. This vision triumphed with positivism, and sanctioned the cumulative results of more than a century of decline of Political Philosophy. Today, on the contrary, we tend to de-sediment the social and to 'reactivate' it by referring it back to the political moment of its originary institution. Now, this process of de-sedimentation is, at the same, time a process of de-totalization of the social. Why is this so? Because, given that society is no longer conceived as unified by an endogenous underlying logic, and given also the contingent character of the acts of political institution, there is no locus from which a sovereign fiat could be pronounced. This constitutive incompletion of the social is crucial to understand the working of hegemonic logics. This is the second dimension of the political: the incompletion of all acts of political institution. Seen from this perspective, the 'politization' of society appears as operating a double displacement: on the one hand there is, certainly, an expansion of the political at the expense of the social; but, on the other hand, politization involves also *contingent* production of the social link and, in this sense, a decentring of society. To put the matter in other terms still: that which makes the political possible – the contingency of the acts of institution – is also what makes it impossible, as ultimately, no instituting act is fully achievable. (This, incidentally, shows the inanity of the argument that sees in the politization of social relations a totalitarian danger. The danger would only exist if the political had a unique centre, a single public sphere which encroached all social spaces.)

Thus, the condition of possibility of something is also its condition of impossibility. As you see, we are already in the terrain of deconstruction. The latter makes possible a crucial turn in Political Theory by: (a) widening the field of structural undecidability; and (b) clearing thus the field for a theory of the decision as taken in an undecidable terrain. As far as the first dimension is concerned, we have the terrain of the undecidables as an ensemble of quasi-transcendental logics (arche-trace, *différance*, supplementarity, iterability, re-mark). This is the field which has been systematically presented by Rodolphe Gasché.[2] As for the second dimension, the very plurality of moves which are possible in that undecidable terrain requires a theory of the decision – an area to which the work of Derrida has been oriented to a considerable extent in recent years.

Undecidability/Decision

I will now successively explore the relevance for politics of these two dimensions of deconstruction – undecidability and decision. Undecidability first. I will broach the discussion by concentrating on the inner logic of three concepts central to contemporary political theory: representation, toleration and power.

1 I have attempted elsewhere[3] to deconstruct the logic of representation. Let me summarize here the main points of my argument. The condition of a good representation is, *apparently*, that there is perfect or transparent transmission, by the representative, of the will of those whom he represents. A good representation would be one in which the will moves in only one direction. This presupposes, of course, that at the point from which the relation of representation starts, there is a full identification

of the represented with his will. The transparency of the relation of representation would be threatened if the will of the representative impinged upon the wills of those that he is supposed to represent. However, what this approach to the problem leaves aside is *why* the relation of representation needs to be established in the first place. The answer is, obviously, that it is because the represented are absent from the place in which the representation takes place, and that decisions affecting them are to be taken there. And these decisions – as any decision – involve negotiations whose result is indeterminate. But this amounts to saying that, if the represented *need* the relation of representation, it is because their identities are incomplete and have to be *supplemented* by the representative. This means that the role of the representative cannot be neutral, and that he will contribute something to the identities of those he represents. *Ergo*, the relation of representation will be, for essential logical reasons, constitutively impure: the movement from represented to representative will necessarily have to be supplemented by a movement in the opposite direction.

Why is this important at all for the understanding of the political working of contemporary societies? The importance lies in that it allows us to understand – as possibilities that are internal to the logic of representation – many developments that had traditionally been considered as perversions or distortions of the representation process. For instance, it has usually been considered that the more democratic a process, the more transparent the transmission of the will of the represented by their representatives. Now, is this *always* the case? No doubt many examples could be quoted in which there has been manipulation of people's will at the hands of their representatives. But there are other instances in which the privileging of the movement from representative to represented is the very condition of democratic participation. In many Third World countries, for example, unemployment and social marginalization leads to shattered social identities at the level of civil society and to situations in which the most difficult thing is how to constitute an *interest*, a *will* to be represented within the political system. In those situations, the task of the popular leaders consists, quite frequently, of providing the marginalized masses with a *language* out of which it becomes possible for them to reconstitute a political identity and a political will. The relation representative → represented has to be privileged as the very condition of a democratic participation and mobilization. In the same way, even in advanced industrial societies, the fragmentation of identities around issue politics requires forms of political aggregation whose constitution involves that political representatives play an active role in the formation of collective wills and not just be the passive mirror of the pre-constituted interests at the level of civil society.

Thus, these internal ambiguities of the relation of representation, the undecidability between the various movements that are possible within it, transform it into the hegemonic battlefield between a plurality of possible decisions. This does not mean that at any time everything that is logically possible becomes, automatically, an actual political possibility. There are inchoated possibilities which are going to be blocked, not because of any logical restriction, but as a result of the historical contexts in which the representative institutions operate. We should not forget, however, that there has been a general tendency to see the historical limitations resulting from those contexts as theoretical limits of the logic of representation as such. From there, there was only one step – which in most cases was unproblematically taken – to transform those limits into a canon and to consider any departure from it as perversion and distortion. All forms of ethnocentrism have developed in the wake of this operation. Deconstruction makes it possible to unknot this link between historical and logical limits and to reinscribe the apparently deviant cases in the very logical structure of the relation under analysis. The result can only be what I do not hesitate to call a widening of the transcendental horizon of politics (and by this I am not only speaking about a cognitive level – changes in performativity necessarily accompany all transcendental change).

2 Let us now move to our second concept, 'toleration'. An identical undecidability can be found within it. In order to be considered as a concept closed in itself, toleration has to exclude that which constitutes its other: intolerance. An unambiguous toleration would be one which has, within itself, no room at all for intolerance. Now, is such a concept of toleration logically achievable? A first answer would be to argue that total, indiscriminate toleration would be self-defeating because: (a) if one accepts tolerating the intolerant beyond a certain limit, one could end up with the installation of an entirely intolerant society under the auspices of toleration; (b) quite apart from the case of the intolerant, there are practices which repugn the moral sense of the community and that most people would agree must not be tolerated. This last statement – which would probably find general assent – confronts us, however, with a new problem. Because it seems now that the condition for toleration to be an unambiguous concept is that we have some normative principle – which cannot be provided by the notion of toleration itself – discriminating between what should and what should not be tolerated. If such a norm could be found, we would have apparently solved our problem, because what has to be tolerated would be unambiguous and certain, even if the abstract category of toleration is unable to provide us with such a criterion of certainty.

This solution, however, fails to deliver the goods. Because it has been able to consolidate the frontier between the tolerable and the intolerable, only by transforming that frontier in the one between the morally acceptable and the morally unacceptable. And this ethical recasting of the issue does much more than grounding toleration: it simply dissolves 'toleration' as a meaningful concept. If what I tolerate is what I morally approve (or, at the very least, that *vis-à-vis* which I am morally neutral) I am not *tolerating* anything. At the most, I am redefining the limits of a perfectly intolerant position. Tolerance only starts when I morally disapprove of something and, however, I accept it. The very condition of approaching the question of toleration is to start realizing that it is not an ethical question at all.

So, when we try to think of the category of 'toleration', we are confronted with two vanishing points: if we try to ground it in itself, without any reference to its contents, it becomes its opposite – intolerance; if we try to ground it in a norm or content different from itself, it dissolves as a meaningful category. But this deadlock already points to the way in which it can be overcome: by inverting the assumptions on which both (inadequate) attempts at solution were based. From the point of view of the content, toleration is a meaningful category if I do not morally agree with what I am tolerating. This requires that I suspend, as far as toleration goes, all kind of ethical judgement on the belief or practice in question. What would be, in that case, the ground for toleration? Simply, the need for society to function in a way that is compatible with a certain degree of internal differentiation. A society that tried to impose a strict conception of the good in all areas of life, would be constantly risking civil war. The neutrality of State institutions *vis-à-vis* rival conceptions of the good is a requirement of any society that has reached a certain level of complexity. But, for the very same reason, if the grounds for toleration are to be found in the viability of a communitarian arrangement, it follows that toleration – i.e. respect for difference – cannot be illimited. An illimited toleration would be as destructive of the social fabric as a totalitarian ethical unification. That is: to be intolerant of some things is the very condition to be tolerant of other. Intolerance is, at the same time, the condition of possibility and impossibility of toleration. We are in the same position as with the category of representation. Where the dividing line between toleration and intolerance will pass is clearly undecidable in terms of the duality toleration/intolerance. As a radical democrat, I am prepared to cope with many more differences than, for instance, a supporter of the moral majority, but these are different decisions taken in an undecidable terrain and, consequently, perfectly compatible with the latter. A hegemonic struggle concerning what should or should not be tolerated is possible, precisely because toleration has no necessary content of its own. What should in any case be clear is that the duality toleration/

intolerance is more basic than each of its two poles – even more: it is the undecidable ground which makes those poles possible.

3 Finally, power. Is power compatible with a free society? A very classical notion of human emancipation presents emancipation and power as antagonistic concepts. A free society, a society reconciled with itself, would be one from which power relations would have been abolished. The very *need* for power would have, in those circumstances, disappeared. It is in those terms that Marxism conceived of the withering away of the State. We can, however, ask ourselves: would such a transparent society be a truly free one? There are serious reasons for doubting it. Freedom involves self-determination and self-determination involves that the will of the self-determined entity is not constrained by anything external to itself. Spinoza knew this well: freedom as self-determination belongs only to God, and the only freedom to which we can aspire is to be conscious of a necessity transcending ourselves. So, we can only be real choosers if the courses of action opened to ourselves are not algorithmically predetermined. Full rationality and possibility of choice are incompatible with each other.

This confronts us with the following paradox: that which limits freedom – i.e. power – is also what makes freedom possible. As in our two previous cases, the condition of possibility of something is also its condition of impossibility. In deciding within an undecidable terrain, I am exercising a power which is, however, the very condition of my freedom. This power presupposes – as all power – the repression of possibilities which are not actualized. This repression is, at the same time, the exercise of my power and the exercise of my freedom. This means that a totally free society – from which power would have been eliminated – and one which would be entirely unfree are equivalent concepts. Power is the shadow of freedom and, as an Arab proverb says, one cannot jump outside one's own shadow. We can certainly free some social possibilities but only at the price of repressing others. The relationship between power and freedom is one of permanent renegotiations and displacement of their mutual frontiers, while the two terms of the equation always remain. Even the most democratic of societies will be the expression of power relations, not of a total or gradual elimination of power.

The last remarks lead us almost naturally to our second aspect: the role that the instance of the decision plays in a deconstructive analysis. Because the structure is undecidable, because there is no possibility of algorithmic closure, the decision cannot be *ultimately* grounded in anything external to itself. As Derrida asserts: 'the moment of *decision, as such,* always remains a finite moment of urgency and precipitation, since it must not be the consequence or the effect of this theoretical or historical moment, of this reflection or this deliberation, since it always marks the interruption of the juridico- or ethico- or politico-cognitive deliberation that precedes it, that *must* precede it. The instance of the decision is a madness, says Kierkegaard.'[4] And, with reference to the just decision, Derrida makes quite clear that the decision exceeds anything containable within a calculable programme:

> The undecidable is not merely the oscillation or the tension between two decisions, it is the experience of that which, though hetero-geneous, foreign to the order of the calculable and the rule, is still obliged – it is of obligation that we must speak – to give itself up to the impossible decision, while taking account of law and rules. A decision that didn't go through the ordeal of the undecidable would not be a free decision, it would only be the programmable application or unfolding of a calculable process.[5]

So, in a first dimension a true decision is something other and more than an effect derived from a calculating rule. A true decision escapes always what any rule can hope to subsume under itself. But a second – and correlative – dimension is that, in that case, the decision has to be grounded in itself, in its own singularity. Now, that singularity cannot bring through the back door what it has excluded from the main entrance – i.e. the universality of the rule. It is simply left to its own singularity. It is because of that that, as Kierkegaard put it, the moment of the decision is the moment of madness.

One possible line of mediation between universality of the rule and singularity of the decision would be through some kind of openness to the otherness of the other, to a primordial ethical experience, in the Levinasian sense. This is the route that Simon Critchley is apparently prepared to take. Mine, however, is different – among other reasons because I do not see in what sense an ethical injunction, even if it only consists of opening oneself to the otherness of the other, can be anything else than a universal principle that precedes and governs any decision. But, in that case, we are apparently in an impasse. Deconstruction, in its first movement, has immensely enlarged the areas of structural unde-cidability, but what the second movement – the logic of the decision taken in an undecidable terrain – would consist of, is far from clear.

I want now to take some tentative steps towards tackling this apparently untractable problem. Let me say that in doing so I speak for myself, and that none of my arguments should be seen as expressing Derrida's position on these issues. As I said at the beginning of this essay, the meaning of my participation in this volume is not so much to engage in an exegesis of Derrida's work – there are others more qualified than myself for that task – as to present what are, in my view, the main consequences of deconstruction and pragmatism for politics. Pursuing this aim I will have to make a detour through a consideration of the logic of the *lack*, which is not present in the deconstructionist tradition. Yet, I have to say in this respect first, that I do not see anything in deconstruction which is logically incompatible with such a detour; and, second, that deconstruction can be very much enriched by a cross-fertilization process with other theoretical traditions – the most relevant for the issue that we are discussing being Lacanian theory.

Decision and the Question of the Subject

1 I will start this task with an assertion that many deconstructionists would, no doubt, object to: in my view, the question of the relationship undecidability/decision cannot properly be approached unless we deal with the question of the subject. Let me refer to the notion of the subject that I have presented in my book *New Reflections on the Revolution of Our Time*.[6] There it is asserted (I am summarizing the argument) that the subject is the distance between the undecidability of the structure and the decision. This thesis is logically connected with another presented in the same essay, according to which dislocation is the trace of contingency within the structure. Let us go briefly through both theses. Dislocation, first. There is dislocation, as deconstructionists well know, not as a result of an empirical imperfection but of something which is inscribed in the very logic of any structure. The argument can be put in these terms: no system can be fully protected given the undecidability of its frontiers (i.e. no system can be a Spinozean eternity); but this is tantamount to saying that identities within that system will be constitutively dislocated and that this dislocation will show their radical contingency. This explains our first thesis: dislocation is the trace of contingency within the structure.

From here we can move straight to the question of the decision. I think that the matter can be put in the following terms. To deconstruct the structure is the same as to show its undecidability, the distance between the plurality of arrangements that are possible out of it and the actual arrangement that has finally prevailed. This we can call a decision in so far as: (a) it is not predetermined by the 'original' terms of the structure; and (b) it requires its passage through the experience of undecidability. The moment of the decision, the moment of madness, is this jump from the experience of undecidability to a creative act, a fiat which requires its passage through that experience. As we have said, this act cannot be explained in terms of any rational underlying mediation. This moment of decision as something left to itself and unable to provide its grounds through any system of rules transcending itself, is the moment of the subject. Why call it a subject? We will approach the matter by considering the constitutive dimensions of any decision worth its name.

The condition for the emergence of the subject (= the decision) is that it cannot be subsumed under any structural determinism, not because he is a substance of his own, but because structural determination – which is the only being that this so-called subject could have – has failed to be its own ground, and it has to be supplemented by contingent interventions. A logic of supplementarity is, in that way, at work, which requires something different from structural determination in order to explain actuality.

This supplement which is a decision *sensu stricto* has a peculiar ontological status: it cannot be a substance of its own (e.g. a self-centred consciousness) and, however, has to be in some way self-determined, because it cannot appeal as its ground to anything different from its own singularity. I would say that we have here something of the nature of a *simulation*. To take a decision is like impersonating God. It is like asserting that one does not have the means of being God, and one has, however, to proceed as if one were Him. The madness of the decision is this blind spot in the structure, in which something totally heterogeneous with it – and, as a result, totally inadequate – has, however, to supplement it.

2 There are here two basic dimensions to be considered, to determine the status of the subject. The first is linked to this operation that I have called 'simulation'. It involves, in the first place, an unbridgeable distance between my lack of being (which is the source of the decision) and that which provides the being that I need in order to act in a world that has failed to construct me as a 'Modification' (*modus*) of itself. Now, this operation of an adventitious acquisition of being has a name which has been haunting contemporary theory – psychoanalytic, in the first place – that name is *identification*. As I have written elsewhere:

> The freedom thus won in relation to the structure is therefore a traumatic fact initially: I am *condemned* to be free, not because I have no structural identity as the existentialists assert, but because I have a *failed* structural identity. This means that the subject is partially self-determined. However, as this self-determination is not the expression of what the subject *already* is but the result of its lack of being instead, self-determination can only proceed through processes of *identification*.[7]

So we can assert that identification is an inherent dimension of the decision. Its presence at the very heart of any decision becomes more visible, the less we can give clear criteria for choosing that with which to identify.

This leads us to our second dimension. We have said before that the systematicity of the system is something that the latter requires, but which is at the same time unachievable. It is, if you want, an object which – as in Kant – shows itself through the impossibility of its adequate representation. Now, what I would like to point out is that the impossibility of an object does not eliminate its need: it continues, as it were, haunting the structure as the presence of its absence. There is something spectral in it, to use a metaphor Derrida is fond of. We can put the matter in a slightly different but equivalent way by saying that if the moment of 'systematicity' is what would close the system within itself, it would constitute the fullness of the system. So, it has to be in some way present in the field of representation but, being an impossible object, its means of representation are going to be constitutively inadequate. This means that whatever assumes that function of representation will be less than that total object and, however (although in a spectral way) will embody it. Through this identity split between an 'ontic' reality and their role of incarnating a fullness totally dissimilar with the former, an imaginary horizon is constituted. Now, let's move back from here to the question of identification. If there is need for identification, it is because there is no identity, in the first place. But in that case, that with which I identify, it is not only its own particular content: it is also one of the names of my absent fullness, the reverse of my original lack. As we see, there is no common measure between the incarnating body and the incarnated object, precisely because the latter is a necessary but also an impossible object. This throws new light on the question of the decision: if the decision presupposes abyssal undecidability and, however, the decision *has* to be taken (there is urgency for the decision, as Derrida puts it), what primarily matters is that there is *a* decision – its actual content being a secondary consideration. This follows from the previously mentioned split, and is the price that we have to pay for impersonating God. God = that who has not to give account of his actions before any tribunal of reason, because He is the source of any rationality. We, 'mortal gods' = those who have to fill the gaps resulting from the absence of God on earth, simulating being Him and replacing with the madness of our decisions an omniscience that will always elude us.

So, why call that chooser a subject? Because the impossibility of a free, substantial subject, of a consciousness identical to itself which is *causa sui*, does not eliminate its need, but just relocates the chooser in the aporetical situation of having to act as if he were a subject, without being endowed with any of the means of a fully fledged subjectivity. The opacity to itself of the decision is other than the names for this ontological condition. It is not possible to do away with the category of 'subject': what it points to is part of the structure of experience. What is possible is to deconstruct it: to show its internal – and unavoidable –

aporias, the undecidable opposites that inhabit it and, in this way, to enlarge the field of the language games that it is possible to play with it.

3 I would like, at this point, to add a precision to my argument. I spoke above, when making reference to structural undecidability, about *abyssal* undecidability. Now, by this slightly exaggerated expression – largely formulated for the sake of the argument – I did not mean that there is a radical absence of rules and that all decision is entirely free. What I meant was that undecidability is a *structured* undecidability, and that what we are always confronted with is a partial destructuration which makes the decision imperative. A situation of total undecidability would be one in which *any* decision would be valid just because it is *a* decision, but in that case we would not have structural undecidables but total absence of structure, and the decision would be made by the chooser in conditions of total omnipotence. What I argue is different, and can be summarized in the following points:

(a) All subject *position* is the effect of a structural determination (or of a rule, which amounts to the same) – there is nothing which is a substantial consciousness constituted outside the structure.

(b) As a structure is, however, constitutively undecidable, decisions are required that the structure (being either a legal code, or an institutional configuration, or family roles, etc.) does not predetermine – this is the moment of the emergence of the *subject* as different from *subject positions*.

(c) As the decision constituting the subject is one taken in conditions of insurmountable undecidability, it is one that does not express the *identity* of the subject (something that the subject *already* is) but requires acts of *identification*.

(d) These acts split the new identity of the subject: this identity is, on the one hand, a particular content, on the other it embodies the absent fullness of the subject.

(e) As this absent fullness is an impossible object, there is no content which is a priori predetermined to fulfil this incarnating function – what object will be privileged by 'politico-cathectic' investments cannot be determined in a context-free situation.

(f) As the decision is always taken within a certain context, what is decidable is not *entirely* free: what counts as a valid decision will have the limits of a structure which, in its actuality, is only partially destructured. The madness of the decision is, if you want, as all madness, a regulated one. The dialectics between social decidables and undecidables is more primary than any unilateralization of the moments of either structural/rule determination, or decision.

So the passage from the universality of the rule to the singularity of the decision and vice versa has to be ensured in some way, although it does not involve either a logical mediation or – I think – an ethical injunction. What makes that passage possible is: (a) the split of the decision between its actual content and that content's function of embodying the absent fullness of the subject. As that fullness has to express itself through contents which have no common measure with it, a plurality of contents will be equally able to assume that function of universal representation. In that way the singularity of the decision will tend to the universality of the rule and vice versa. It is the indeterminacy of the content through which the universal finds its expression, what differentiates this passage from a dialectical mediation. But if in this first movement the compatibility between universality of the rule and indeterminacy of the singular enlarges the field of the contents which can embody that universal function, we have (b) a movement of the opposite sign, as far as contexts that *factually* limit structural undecidability, limit also the range of the contents which can, at any given moment, play that role of universal representation. It could be argued that with this I am not actually proposing a fully fledged concept of the passage between singularity and universality, but just *limiting* the terrain within which that passage can take place. This is true, but my answer is that this is the most one can do. The highest form of rationality that society can reach is that of a regulated madness.

If this is the only kind of passage that I think is possible between structural undecidability and decision, it is clear that for me that passage cannot have an ethical grounding. This is not the result of any ethical insensitivity on my part, but of the conviction that nothing ethical can be derived from the general structure of experience. I am definitely against contemporary currents which tend to an 'ethicization' of onto-logical levels. There are, in my view, no ethical principles or norms whose validity is independent of all communitarian spaces.

The problem of the political is different. For if the political is not conceived in its current narrow sense, but, instead, as the process of *institution* of the social, it is clear that this instituting moment becomes one with the question of the relation undecidability/decision that we have been discussing. Deconstruction is a primarily *political* logic in the sense that, by showing the structural undecidability of increasingly larger areas of the social, it also expands the area of operation of the various moments of political institution. This does not imply, certainly, that one can derive, from deconstructive premises, a decision about concrete political arrangements in a particular situation; but we can, yet, derive something concerning the form of the political as such, whatever its contents. The central theme of deconstruction is the politico-discursive production of society. I will illustrate what I mean with reference to two examples. The first concerns 'hegemony' which is for me, as I have anticipated, the central category in thinking the political; the second, 'democracy'.

4 We have seen that the absent fullness of the structure (of the community in this case) has to be represented/misrepresented by one of its particular contents (a political force, a class, a group). This relation by which a particular element assumes the impossible task of a universal representation, is what I call a *hegemonic* relation. It is because of this constitutive split between singularity and universality – this tendency of a signifier to evade its strict attachment to a signified while keeping a ghostly relation to it – that politics is possible at all. Otherwise, there would be only a blind clash between impenetrable social forces. It is because the particularity of the decision assumes the function of an imaginary closure – while not being entirely able to perform an actual and final closure – that no blind clash exists but, instead, a reciprocal contamination between the universal and the singular or, rather, the never ending and never totally convincing impersonation of the former by the latter.

5 Second, democracy. Once again, I am not saying that democracy is the manifest destiny of deconstruction. Theoretical and political arguments that take deconstruction as their starting point can go in *many* directions. But it is possible, however, to show how, if one starts from democratic theory at its present stage, deconstruction helps to radicalize some of its trends and arguments. Let us return once more to the contingent and unstable relationship between fullness of the community and its singular and transient forms of incarnation. If the fullness of the community had found its *true* body, no democratic competition between forces attempting to incarnate that fullness would be possible. The rationality of the only one possible choice would make a joke of the very notion of choice. The perverse logic of the 'love at first sight' would make any dialectics of love impossible. But if the logic of love, rationality, fullness always reactivates the gap between empty (although necessary) universality and the bodies incarnating it, democracy, as the ambiguous practice of trying to fill that gap while keeping it permanently open, would have found its conditions of possibility. Undecidability and decision are the names of that ineradicable and constitutive tension which makes possible a *political* society.

To summarize: deconstruction and hegemony are the two essential dimensions of a single theoretico-practical operation. Hegemony requires deconstruction: without the radical structural undecidability that the deconstructive intervention brings about, many strata of social relations would appear as essentially linked by necessary logics and there would be nothing to hegemonize. But deconstruction also requires hegemony, that is, a theory of the decision taken in an undecidable terrain: without a theory of the decision, that distance between structural undecidability and actuality would remain untheorized. But that decision can *only* be a hegemonic one – i.e. one that (a) is self-grounded; (b) is exclusionary, as far as it involves the repression of alternative decisions; and (c) is internally split, because it is both *this* decision but also *a* decision. For reasons that I have tried to make clear, the self-grounded character of the decision leads us to the subject as subject of the lack, its exclusionary dimension to an ontological primacy of politics (of the acts of political institution); and its internal split, to its specifically hegemonic status.

Rorty's Pragmatism

As far as Rorty's pragmatism is concerned, my agreements and disagreements are of a different nature. Let me start with a point in which I definitely endorse Rorty's position: I certainly subscribe to his assertion that there is no room for ethics to provide any kind of 'post'-metaphysical, but still 'first philosophy', grounding. There is with Rorty no danger of any kind of Levinasian proclivity. For reasons outlined above, I agree with Rorty that ethical values are only 'conversationally' grounded – that is (in my own terms) socially and discursively constructed. I do not see any reason to attribute to ethical values (or to a primary experience of the alterity of the other) any foundational role. From the point of view we were discussing earlier – that of the decision – this means, of course, that the radical lack of foundation cannot be ultimately filled, that there is no final bridge between universality and singularity, and that any attempt at mediation between them – ethical or of any other kind – is a blind alley.

Yet, once this general agreement with Rorty has been established, the points in which my approach diverges from his are only too visible. Between what I call 'discursive-hegemonic construction' and Rorty's 'conversationalism', the points of divergence are at least as important as those of convergence. The latter exist because, in both cases, we are dealing with non-foundationalist constructions of meaning, but the idea of a 'conversational' grounding seems to add the further assumption of a necessarily peaceful process, as if the non-foundational nature of the grounding involved the 'civilized' character of the exchange. Now, this does not follow at all. What is certainly excluded from that kind of grounding is a rationalist terrorism which would draw from its algorithmic certainty a radical intolerance *vis-à-vis* any divergent opinion. But, beyond that, we cannot deduce anything else about the nature of the exchange. The process of persuasion, for instance, can be the result of demagogic pressures, without the latter having to appeal to any kind of foundationalist principle. I think that what Rorty has not explored enough is the range of possible practices which are compatible with his 'redescriptive grounding', and has attached the latter too quickly to a 'conversationalism' which is certainly akin to his liberal preferences, but that it is only *one* of the language games which it is possible to play within his historicist and nominalist viewpoint.

This points to the general line of the objections that I want to put to Rorty. These objections have nothing to do with his basic pragmatistic outlook – a terrain in which I do not find myself too far from him – but rather with his unilateralization of the results of that pragmatism. To put it bluntly: I think that if he wants to ground on pragmatist premises the concrete politics that he advocates, something intermediate is missing. I will make three basic points in this respect.

1 The first concerns the area to which the effects of Rorty's pragmatism applies. Is pragmatism a point of vantage from which one can illuminate what has *always* been the case, or is it, instead, the source of pure self-referential effects? To put it in other terms: has history always proceeded through pragmatic redescriptions, or are the latter the effect of the introduction of pragmatist premises? When he points out, for instance, that one of the basic mutations of the last two hundred years is the increasing realization that truth is fabricated rather than found, are we to understand his assertion as meaning that this has always been the case, even before that increasing realization, or that the realization coincided with the beginning of the fact – i.e. that before the realization, truth was found rather than fabricated? This is, of course, a rhetorical question, because I do not think for a moment that Rorty's answer would be for the second alternative. If I do not think, however, that mine is an otiose question, it is because of the consequences that follow from fully developing the implications of the first alternative. If, to start with, intellectual history – or history *tout court* – has always proceeded through pragmatic redescriptions, it is our task as students of the past to bring to the surface the conceptual – or extra-conceptual – devices through which pragmatists *malgré eux* such as Plato, Leibnitz or Hegel were employing when they were engaged in the construction of rational-istic systems. This is certainly a most useful and fascinating task but, in carrying it out, is not our pragmatist doing something quite similar to what, in other intellectual traditions we would call *to deconstruct* a text? There is certainly nothing wrong in this intellectual convergence except that, if it is pushed beyond a certain point, it starts to jeopardize *some* of the political consequences that Rorty wants to derive from his pragmat-istic premises.

I see that matter this way. If pragmatic redescription is all there has been in history – and I do not back down from this conclusion – Rorty has to show in what way not only Dewey, James or Wittgenstein have been engaged in pragmatic games, but also all kind of metaphysicians and dogmatic politicians who claimed to be doing exactly the opposite. Pragmatism becomes, in that way, something like an intellectual horizon allowing us to redescribe all currents of thought and all events in history. In that case, however, we cannot derive from pragmatistic premises any particular politics (in the same way that, as I have argued, one cannot derive a democratic politics from purely deconstructive premises). The only possibility of welding Rorty's liberalism and his pragmatism would be to present today's liberalism as the moment of the full awareness of what is involved in pragmatism, and the ensemble of past history as the imperfect and provisional steps leading to that awareness. But this kind of 'philosophy of history' approach – apart from still requiring to show the logical connection between the two components of the awareness – flies in the face of the whole of Rorty's intellectual enterprise.

2 Conversely, we could argue that, in the same way that we can deconstruct any text by showing its underlying (and concealed) pragmatic strategies, we can also, starting from explicit pragmatistic premises (although, of course, not only from them) construct a politics very different from Rorty's. There is nothing in pragmatism that necessarily restricts it to the kind of liberal piecemeal engineering advocated by Rorty. Pragmatism as an intellectual gesture liberates many more possibilities and courses of development than Rorty is actually prepared to recognize. To start with, our three categories previously discussed – toleration, representation, power – are as we said, not conceptually closed in themselves. They are the starting point of a plurality of possible lines of development, and if the latter do not prescribe any necessary choice, what are we facing but the pragmatic terrain of a 'social construction of reality'? In the same way, a concept like 'hegemony' points to a logic which can very well be described in pragmatist terms. Gramsci was breaking with a conception according to which there were aprioristic laws of capitalism imposing and dictating a necessary course to historical events. Against it he asserted what has been described as the primacy of politics: the pragmatic formation of collective wills through contingent articulations whose success was entirely context-dependent. This is a politics very different from Rorty's, but perfectly compatible with pragmatistic premises.

So, the problem that I see in Rorty's formulations is that he tries to weld his liberalism and his pragmatism without reckoning enough with the fact that the latter does not necessarily lead to the former. The fact that revolutionary transformations have been justified through foundationalist discourses does not entail that the abandonment of those discourses leads automatically to a politics of piecemeal engineering from which all antagonism and social division have been eradicated. If it leads to something – given the proliferation of conflicts in the world in which we live – it is to ask ourselves what are the discursive conditions for a pragmatic construction of such antagonisms and social divisions. Of course, Rorty is entitled to prefer a politics of piecemeal engineering – what Saint-Simon called a transition from the government of men to the administration of things – but what he cannot legitimately do is to ground his preference in a simple transition from foundationalism to pragmatism.

This illegitimate transition from stating the case for pragmatism (in which I am largely prepared to follow Rorty) to deriving from that case the advocacy of a particular type of politics (in which I am not prepared to do so) can be seen reflected in the ambiguous use of some terms which are very much part of either Rorty's vocabulary or of the vocabulary with which his enterprise has been frequently described. One of these descriptions is that he proceeds to a *banalization* of the language of politics. Now this can mean two things. One is that the sublimity of the public sphere, as the one which would have an ontological privilege in the construction of the social, has to be ruined. About this, I cannot agree more with Rorty. In the same way as psychoanalysis, as deconstruction, the task of pragmatism is to subvert all sublimity by showing the 'ignoble origins' in which it is rooted. But what is understood by banalization is frequently something very different: the attempt to (a) assert that the phenomena associated with that sublimity have to disappear from the political sphere; (b) reduce – in an anti-intellectualistic way – the language of political analysis to the ordinary language used in political exchanges in the 'rich democracies' of the West.

Now, I do not go at all along with these two operations. As far as the first is concerned, to show the pragmatic roots of something is not the same thing as to disqualify that something. Many people can pin their hopes and their emotional investments in a particular political aim, and the fact that those hopes are the result of a complex discursive-hegemonic construction and not the expression of an aprioristic essence, is no argument against their validity. As far as the second attempt is concerned, there is no reason, if one starts from pragmatistic premises, either to reduce political language to the actual language used in political exchanges in the West, or – even less – to assume that the study of this language cannot go beyond the actual categories that it employs. I will only say, first, that if social life constantly requires – according to Rortyian premises – the production of new vocabularies, why should *political* languages be excluded from this general rule? And, second, that if the analysis of the logic of an argumentative process shows us something more than what the latter explicitly asserts, I do not see how this showing would be possible unless we describe the 'grammar' of this argumentation process with categories different from those contained in the 'language object'. It is not, of course, that I am taking a dogmatic 'metalinguistic' position but, rather, that there is something we can call a discursive metalinguistic operation, whose premises and loci of enunciation have to be pragmatically determined. Otherwise we would have to say that psychoanalysis is wrong because the unconscious does not use its categories.

A second example is 'irony'. Again, there is one dimension in the Rortyian use of this term to which I would subscribe: that alluding to an absence of foundation which creates a gap or distance between strong belief and rational underpinning of that belief. But the very word used – irony – seems to link the experience of that gap to some sort of offhandish detachment. This is an unacceptable reduction which eludes the plurality of psychological negotiations of that gap – these negotiations being one of the central problems of politics. I asked Rorty once, in a public discussion, if he thought 'irony' was the adequate term to describe the moral courage of somebody who is confronted with Auschwitz and, however, resists it without seeking consolation in fundamentalist dreams. Rorty's answer was 'no'. I agree with that answer and I would generalize the argument by asserting that one of the tasks of both political theory and political practice is – rather than remaining fixated in the figure of the 'ironist' – to explore the whole gamut of strategies or language games through which the presence/absence of that gap is, all the time, socially negotiated.

3 A final remark. One of the difficulties of Rorty's discourse is that one is never entirely clear about the theoretical status of the basic distinctions which govern its categories. How is, for instance, the key distinction between the public and the private actually established? One does not actually know. All we are told is that there is some kind of incommensurability between the (private) demands of self-creation, and those (public) of human solidarity, but the nature of the partition is never theorized. This distinction should not necessarily be one of essence; it could perfectly well be recast in historicist terms – specifying, for instance, the pragmatic operations through which it came into existence in the first place. But about this the text of Rorty is silent. Yet, I do not see how a pragmatist discourse can do without explaining the genesis of the distinction. A discourse of pure fiat, one which limits itself to stating the distinction without any concern with its actual genesis, can only be a transcendental discourse – one that Rorty, I am sure, would do anything in his power to avoid. And, however, how to deny a transcendental status to the distinction if the only language game we can play with it is to state its validity as a criterion demarcating two

entirely different areas of experience? If, on the contrary, we inscribe the distinction itself in the patchy and complex history of its production – something that any consequent pragmatist should do – we are confronted with a rather different scenario: the distinction itself becomes problematic and reveals itself as what it actually is – just an ideal-typical attempt at stabilizing an essentially unstable frontier which is constantly trespassed and overflown by movements coming from its two sides: personal self-realization investing public aims, politization of the private sphere, private aims whose fulfilment requires legal recognition, etc. Only in a tidy rationalistic world can the demands of self-realization and those of human solidarity be so neatly differentiated as Rorty wants them to be.

I think that the merit of Rorty is to have reinscribed the problematic of American Pragmatism within the wider field of the critique of the Enlightenment and the general discussion concerning the limits of modernity. It is certainly through this reinscription that a multitude of pragmatist themes can develop their full subversive and creative potential. Conversely, the limitation of Rorty's approach – as it has been developed so far – is that he has accepted at face value the politico-theoretical articulation of themes coming from liberalism, as if that articulation could not be, in turn, deconstructed. For here the process should move in both directions: if the pragmatist reading of the tradition of the Enlightenment can act as a fruitful corrosive of the latter, the tradition of Continental thought can react, in turn, by helping to shake some of the comfortable assumption of American liberalism.

Conclusion

Let me finish this essay with a few considerations concerning the potential relevance of both pragmatism and deconstruction for the understanding of the transformed scenario of politics at the end of this century. If we turn our attention to the classical forms of reflection on the nature of political interaction, we could say that they have been dominated – as far as normativity is concerned – by the attempt to make that interaction unnecessary, or at least to reduce it to a subordinated position, whose boundaries had to be clearly delimited and its possible excesses carefully monitored. Solving the question of politics largely consisted in finding the conditions of a social functioning from which any indeterminacy or ambiguity in the structuration of the community – especially the disruptive effects of antagonisms and social division – would be either eliminated or strictly regulated. What political reflection tried to achieve was, to a large extent, to find the means of eliminating politics, if by the latter we understand a type of practice which puts into question the meaning of social structures and institutions and makes it dependent on the outcome of contingent strategic moves.

For strategy is at the heart of any action which can be called political. Strategy involves, in an indissociable synthesis, a moment of articulation – the institution of the social; a moment of contingency, as far as that institution is only one among those that are possible in a given context; and a moment of antagonism – the institution being only possible through a hegemonic victory over conflicting wills. Now, political theory was, to a large extent, an effort to circumvent this strategic moment and to limit the effects that it could have over the process of social reproduction. For ancient ontology (Plato being its most accomplished expression) the ruler is not a strategist but the one who *knows* – i.e. not the one who institutes the community as an expression of his wisdom, but who recognizes what the community essentially is, prior to any deliberation or calculation. For Christianity the communal order is instituted by God, and escapes the contingency of any purely human construction. For Hobbes, the covenant that surrenders all sovereignty to the ruler, sanctions the death of politics. For liberalism, individual rights do not open the way to strategic thinking, for the plurality of the starting point is offset by social mechanisms which escape all politico-strategic control – the 'invisible hand' being the most obvious one. Even in the case of democracy, which avoided any dogmatic postulation of a common good and instituted the locus of power as an empty place, a complicated dialectic between democratic values and democratic procedures prevented democratic logic from fully developing its subversive strategic potential. The line initiated by Machiavelli, who made substantive values dependent on strategic calculation, had a rather marginal presence in modern political thought. It is only in the con-temporary world – where the effects of globalization, rapid and multi-directional change and social fragmentation are making social structures less sedimented and increasingly dependent on iniatives taken from multiple points of the social fabric – that the preconditions for a general-ization of strategic thinking have obtained. This has also put into question the ontological presuppositions of classical political theory.

Now, in the search for forms of thought/action which operated in this widened strategic field, both deconstruction and pragmatism represent important steps forward. In both cases the foundationalism of classical political theory is put into question; in both cases structural undecidability leads back to acts of decision which are self-grounding; in both cases the contingency of these acts of decision opens the possibility of conceiving any actual political order as having a purely hegemonic and transient foundation. For this liberating effect to develop freely, it is however necessary that both currents of thought manage to avoid some of the dangers that could deviate them from their route: in the case of deconstruc-tion, as we have seen, the danger is what I have called the 'ethicization' of the ontological levels, the tendency to revert, on ethical grounds, to a discourse of *'first'* philosophy; in the case of pragmatism – at least in its Rortyian version – the danger is some sort of parochialism – its reduction to only those strategic moves that are possible within the discursive universe of American liberalism. If these pitfalls are, however, avoided, the question that looms on the horizon is this: are we really *applying* deconstruction and pragmatism to the political field or, rather, by radicalizing their respective logics are we unveiling their ultimately political nature? I think that, despite its apparent simplicity, the very *possibility* of this question illuminates central aspects of the politico-intellectual crossroads at which we are today located.

Notes

1 Cf. Ernesto Laclau and Chantal Mouffe, *Hegemony and Socialist Strategy. Towards a Radical Democratic Politics*, London, Verso, 1985; and Ernesto Laclau, *New Reflections on the Revolution of Our Time*, London, Verso, 1990.
2 Rodolphe Gasché, *The Tain of the Mirror. Derrida and the Philosophy of Reflection*, Cambridge, Mass., Harvard University Press, 1986.
3 Ernesto Laclau, 'Power and Representation', in Mark Poster (ed.), *Politics, Theory and Contemporary Culture*, New York, Columbia Univeristy Press, 1993, pp. 277–96.
4 Jacques Derrida, 'Force of Law: The "Mystical Foundation of Authority"', in Drucilla Cornell, Michel Rosenfeld and David Gray Carlson (eds), *Deconstruction and the Possibility of Justice*, New York and London, Routledge, 1992.
5 *Ibid.*
6 Ernesto Laclau, *New Reflections on the Revolution of our Time*, London, Verso, 1990, pp. 41–5.
7 *Ibid.*, p. 44.

6

Response to Ernesto Laclau

Richard Rorty

In my remarks earlier in this volume (see Chapter 2) I said that I did not think that deconstruction had done much either for the study of literature or for a grasp of our political problems – not because deconstruction is bad philosophy, but because we should not expect too much of philosophy. We should not ask philosophy, of whatever sort, to accomplish tasks for which it is unsuited. Although I have learned a great deal from Laclau's writings, I nevertheless think of him as overestimating Derrida's political utility, and thereby contributing to an unfortunate over-philosophication of leftist political debate. That over-philosophication has helped create, in the universities of the US and Britain (where Derrida's, Laclau's, and Chantal Mouffe's books are very widely read and admired) a self-involved academic left which has become increasingly irrelevant to substantive political discussion.

Such over-philosophication is evinced when Laclau isolates notions like 'toleration' or 'the political' or 'representation' and then points out that we cannot, simply by thinking about that notion, figure out what to do. Who except for a few wacky hyperrationalists, ever thought we could? Who takes seriously the idea that an idea, or notion, or principle, could contain the criteria of its own correct application?

Laclau says that 'because the structure is undecidable, because there is no possibility of algorithmic closure, the decision cannot be *ultimately* grounded in anything external to itself'. He thereby reinstates the old reason-vs.-will, algorithm-vs.-arbitrary choice, distinction. The idea that there is no middle ground between algorithms and 'ultimately groundless' acts of will lay behind the Vienna Circle's insistence that what wasn't determinable in advance by rules was 'cognitively meaningless'. As Laclau's citation of Kierkegaard's 'the instance of the decision is a madness' suggests, it also lay behind the existentialists' suggestion that if you don't have a knock-down argument in favour of a decision, that decision somehow swings free of all rational activity.[1]

I see no reason to rehabilitate this common denominator of rationalism and existentialism. Doing so will simply keep the pendulum swinging between these two unhelpful positions. Granted that decision is not deliberation, it seems to me misleading to say, with Derrida and Laclau, that 'decision always *interrupts* deliberation'. That suggests a picture of Will swooping down and taking matters out of Reason's hands. It is more plausible to describe decision as we normally do, as the *outcome* of deliberation – even when we are quite aware that equally rational deliberation might have led us to a different decision. Wittgenstein has taught us that the fact that anything can be made out to be in conformity with a rule does not mean that rules are useless, nor that decisions cannot be made in conformity with them.

I see little resemblance between taking a decision and (in Laclau's phrase) 'impersonating God', if only because we do the former, but not the latter, dozens of times a day. Nor do I see that the content of a decision has, as Laclau puts it, 'the function of embodying the absent fullness of the subject'. I can see that it might be so described if one were interested in constructing a philosophical or psychoanalytic theory of selfhood in terms of a dialectic of presence and absence. But I doubt that such a theory could be of any help in thinking about politics.[2]

To be a bit more concrete, consider Laclau's example of political representation. I see the election of representatives to govern a population which is too large, or too spread out, to get together in a town meeting as a sensible practical expedient. Every polity that resorts to this expedient is aware that the decisions taken by the representatives may not be those which would have been taken by a gathering of the entire citizenry. But I do not see that this situation is clarified by the claim that 'the relation of representation will be, for essential logical reasons ... constitutively impure.'

Laclau thinks that putting the matter in these terms *is* clarificatory, because

> it allows us to understand – as possibilities that are internal to the logic of representation – many developments that had traditionally been considered perversions or distortions of the representative process. For instance, it has usually been considered that the more democratic a process, the more transparent the transmission of the will of the represented by their representatives.

But *is* this in fact the usual view? Ever since we started electing representatives, many of them have said (as J.S. Mill said to the electors of Westminster) that their job is to make better decisions than the electors could make for themselves. The question of just how transparent representation should be has always been on the table. The answer to this question has varied, and should vary, with a host of local factors (level of general literacy, degree of complexity of the laws, etc.). Philosophy has not contributed much, and probably cannot contribute much, to the choice between alternative answers.

Laclau goes on to say that 'these internal ambiguities of the relation of representation ... transform it into the hegemonic battlefield between a plurality of possible decisions'. Why 'transform'? What, in ethical and political deliberation, *isn't* always already a battlefield between a plurality of possible decisions? Does it help to explain the existence of such battlefields by referring to the internal ambiguities of a concept? What do we get, other than a higher level of abstraction, from using such terms and thereby (as Laclau puts it) 'widening the transcendental horizon of politics'? Isn't Laclau just telling us, in elevated language, what we already knew: that elected representatives often should not decide how to vote simply by asking their constituents how they would vote?

I have nothing against higher levels of abstraction. They often come in handy. But I think that the pressure to rise to a higher level of abstraction should, so to speak, come from below. Locally useful abstractions ought to emerge out of local and banal political deliberations. They should not be purveyed ready-made by philosophers, who tend to take the jargon of their own discipline too seriously. Unless you were already familiar with Kant's and Hegel's use of *Grund*, it would never occur to you to try to 'ground the concept [of tolerance] in itself' or to ground it in 'a norm or content different from itself'.

Consider an analogy. Although some mathematics is obviously very useful to engineers, there is a lot of mathematics that isn't. Mathematics outruns engineering pretty quickly, and starts playing with itself. Philosophy, we might say, outruns politics ('social engineering,' as it is sometimes called) pretty quickly, and also starts playing with itself. (Consider the train of thought which took Plato from the genuine political questions of the *Republic* to the ingenious and amusing versions of solitaire developed in the *Parmenides*.) I suspect the notion of 'condition of possibility and impossibility' is as useless to political deliberation as Cantorean diagonalization is to civil engineers. Surely the burden is on those who, like Laclau, think the former useful to explain just how and where the utility appears, rather than taking it for granted?

It is of course true that engineering is always catching up with mathematics – using mathematical concepts in desperate earnest which had been dreamed up just for fun, and with no thought of being applied to anything. Transcendental numbers were once of no interest in engineers, but they are now. So how can we tell in advance whether or not transcendental conditions will be of interest to the electorate, their representatives, and onlooking kibitzers (like Laclau and me) on the political process?

We cannot, of course. Still, we should notice that the demand for more information about transcendental numbers, information which turned out to be purveyable by mathematicians in ready-made form, emerged from below, as engineers became more ambitious and courageous. The mathematicians were not in a position to predict the utility which their inventions turned out to have. Nor did they have the skills and information required to predict when and how a demand for their products might emerge.

Fans of Cantor's diagonalization method did not assume that there *should* be such a demand (from, for example, people trying to forestall flash flooding). Hegelians of both the left and the right, however, have assumed that certain notions – notions which will remain pretty much unintelligible unless one has read some Hegel – *should* be found useful (by, for example, people trying to forestall dictatorship).

Dewey complained at length about the prevalence of this assumption. 'We need guidance', he said:

> in dealing with particular perplexities in domestic life, and we are met by dissertations on the Family or by assertions of the sacredness of the individual Personality. We want to know about the worth of the institution of private property as it operates under given conditions of definite time and place. We meet with the reply of Proudhon that property generally is theft, or with that of Hegel that the realization of will is the end of all institutions, and that private ownership as the mastery of personality over physical nature is a necessary element in such realization. Both answers may have a certain suggestiveness in connection with specific situations. But the conceptions are not proffered for what they may be worth in connection with special historic phenomena. They are general answers supposed to have a universal meaning that covers and dominates all particulars. Hence they do not assist inquiry. They close it.[3]

My reaction to Laclau's use of Derridean notions is similar to Dewey's reaction to T.H. Green's use of Hegelian notions. The twist Laclau puts on Derrida may, indeed, 'have a certain suggestiveness in connection with specific situations'. But we shall have to wait and see whether it in fact does.

To illustrate my doubts about whether it will, consider Laclau's claim that 'the duality toleration/intolerance is more basic than each of its two poles – even more: it is the undecidable ground which makes those poles possible.' I cannot figure out how to make this point suggest anything about (to use the example of a political issue which happens to be urgent in my own country at the present moment) whether civilian authorities should be tolerant of the frequent intolerance of soldiers for their homo-sexual comrades-in-arms. I do not think that they should, but when I argue for this view with people on the other side of the issue, we never reach the level of abstraction at which Laclau is operating.

I agree that if we did not have a contrast effect (tolerance/intolerance, dark/light, etc.) we should have no use for either of the terms used to contrast with one another. In that rather uninteresting sense, I agree that a contrastive duality is always 'more basic' than either of its terms, and even, if you like, that 'it makes them possible'. But I do not see what 'undecidable ground' adds. I am glad to have learned (from Saussure and Wittgenstein) that Locke was wrong in thinking of words as names of discrete ideas, that the meaning of a word is its use in the language, and that words have the uses they do because of the possibility of using other, contrasting terms. But I see no way to make this new and improved philosophy of language relevant to my reflections on how political deliberations are, or should be, conducted. A theory of meaning seems as irrelevant here as a theory of a priori knowledge – *différance* as irrelevant as *Grund*; Saussure and Derrida as irrelevant as Kant and Hegel.

Laclau and I of course agree that 'language is a system of differences', but we diverge when he says that 'this systematicity depends ... on establishing the limits of the system, and this requires delimitation from what is beyond those limits'. I have no idea of what the limits of the system of differences which is language are, nor of how it could possibly have any. I agree that 'no system can be fully protected given the undecidability of its frontiers', and would cite Wittgenstein's arguments about rule-following in support of this point. But I do not see that the 'contingency' which this unprotectedness produces is anything to worry about. All this contingency comes to is, once again, the banal fact that there are no algorithms for deciding controversial questions (about what we mean, what we should say, what follows from what, and the like).

Turning now to Laclau's discussion of my own views, I quite agree with him that peaceful conversation 'is only *one* of the language games which it is possible to play within his historicist and nominalist viewpoint'. I can cheerfully grant this point because I do *not* 'want to ground on pragmatist premises the concrete politics' I advocate, nor do I think that today's liberalism is 'the moment of full awareness of what is involved in pragmatism'. On the contrary, as I have said above, I doubt that philo-sophy (even pragmatist philosophy) is ever going to be very useful for politics, and am quite sure that whatever utility it may have will be (as Dewey said) a matter of occasional suggestiveness rather than of 'grounding'.

Do I, as Laclau says I do, try to weld my liberalism and my pragmatism? Only to the following extent: I think that both are expressions of, and reinforce, the same sort of suspicion of religion and metaphysics. Both can be traced back to some of the same historical causes (religious tolerance, constitutional democracy, Darwin). This is not a very tight weld, but I am not interested in making it any tighter.

Laclau queries my use of the terms 'banalization' and 'irony'. As for banalization, I agree with Laclau that 'there is no reason, if one starts from pragmatistic premises, either to reduce political language to the actual language used in political exchanges in the West, or . . . to assume that the study of this language cannot go beyond the actual categories it employs.' But, in the first place, the actual language used in such exchanges has been constantly changing, without much help from philosophy. (Consider terms like 'welfare state' and 'environmental protection', which are banal and unphilosophical, but relatively new and very useful.) In the second place, nobody who studies a language uses only the terms of the language studied; they always use some 'second-order', heuristic expressions. The issue which separates me from Laclau is not how banal it is best to be, but the extent to which Derrida's philosophy suggests some useful new language *either* for first-order, deliberative, *or* second-order, kibitzing purposes.

As for 'irony', Laclau is certainly right that this term is not a suitable description of moral courage. Yet it seemed a reasonable choice for describing what I called, in *Contingency, Irony and Solidarity,* an appreciation of the contingency of final vocabularies. I admit, however, that the word does have overtones of what Laclau calls 'offhandish detachment', so perhaps it was a bad choice. Still, now I'm stuck with it. So all I can do is remind people of my definition, and ask them to ignore the irrelevant overtones.

Towards the end of his essay, Laclau says that I am never entirely clear about the theoretical status of distinctions like public-vs.-private. This is because I am unclear about the utility of the notion of 'theoretical status'. I have never been able to make sense of the claim that something has been 'inadequately theorized'. As a good pragmatist, I think that theories are like tools: you only reach for them when there is a specific problem to be solved. There is no criterion of inadequacy of theorization apart from the specification of such a problem.

I do not see how to 'theorize' the nature of the partition between the private and the public, except to say that by 'the private' I mean the part of life in which we carry out our duties to ourselves, and do not worry about the effects of our actions on others. By the public I mean the part in which we do worry about such effects. I see what Laclau means when he says that this is 'an ideal-typical attempt at stabilizing an essentially unstable frontier which is constantly trespassed and overflown', but I should protest that I really wasn't interested in *stabilizing* anything. I was only trying to remind my readers that sometimes philosophy (even the most inspired and original sort of philosophy – like Kierkegaard's or Derrida's) can, like art and literature, have uses which are pretty much irrelevant to our moral and political responsibilities to other people. It is sometimes useful to remind people of a plausible distinction, without trying either to stabilize a frontier or to theorize a partition.

I agree with Laclau about the respective dangers of deconstruction and pragmatism – namely, too much reversion to the discourse of 'first' philosophy in the one case and too much parochial all-Americanism in the other. But, predictibly enough, the first danger is more obvious to me than the second. I think that the level of abstraction to which Laclau ascends in order to kibitz on contemporary politics is too high – too reminiscent of 'first' philosophy. I see Laclau as continuing a tradition that began with Marx, and was encouraged by Lenin's claim that you need to study Hegel before you can grasp your time in thought (not to mention Althusser's claim that Marx gave us a 'science').

I think that it was a misfortune for the left that Marx, a brilliant political economist, happened to have taken a degree in philosophy when he was young. I also think that it is a misfortune for philosophers that their leftist admirers keep trying to make them relevant to the contemporary political situation.[4] I see it as an advantage of American political thought that the philosophical side of Marx was never taken very seriously by American intellectuals. I think that Rawls is a good example of what I commended above – answering a demand for theorization from below, and meeting that demand with a minimal amount of first philosophy. I applaud Rawls's remark that, for the purposes of formulating a political theory of justice, it is best to 'stay on the surface, philosophically speaking'.

I realize that these views reflect what Laclau calls 'the comfortable assumptions of American liberalism', and may be highly parochial. But there is, it seems to me a parallel European (and, more specifically, French) parochialism – one which rests on equally comfortable assumptions. Perhaps the best Laclau and I can do is to keep on reminding each other of the dangers of these two forms of parochialism.

Notes

1 This idea also lies behind the complaints of cultural conservatives that if you follow dangerous 'irrationalists', you make morals and politics a mere struggle for power. See John Searle's citation of Kuhn, Derrida and myself as foes of 'the Western Rationalistic Tradition' in his 'Rationality and Realism: What Is At Stake?' (*Daedalus*, vol. 122, no. 4 (Fall 1992), pp. 55–84. I reply to this article in my 'Does Academic Freedom Have Philosophical Presuppositions?', *Academe* 80, no. 6 (November/December 1994), pp. 52–63.

2 I am confirmed in this view that an account of the deep nature of the self does not make contact with politics by reading Slavoj Zizek's remarks on political liberalism (and on my own work) in Chapter 9 of his *Looking Awry* (Cambridge,

Mass., MIT Press, 1991). Zizek starts off from a Lacanian account of desire, and says that 'The problem with this liberal dream is that the split between the public and private never comes about without a certain remainder' and that 'the very domain of the public law is "smeared" by an obscure dimension of "private" enjoyment' (p. 159). He goes on to 'locate in a precise manner the flaw of Rorty's "liberal utopia": It presupposes the possibility of a universal social law *not* smudged by a "pathological" stain of enjoyment, i.e., delivered from the superego dimension.'

I do not see that political liberalism need presuppose anything of the sort. I imagine that *ressentiment*, as well as the mild form of sadism which is intrinsic to Kantian notions of obligation, will go on forever – or at least as long as there are judges, police, etc. But I should think the question is whether anybody has any better ideas for a legal and political system than the liberal, constitutional, social democratic one. I can find nothing in Freud, Lacan, Zizek, Derrida, Laclau or Mouffe which persuades me that anybody does.

3 John Dewey, *Reconstruction in Philosophy*, (The Middle Works of John Dewey), vol. 12, Carbondale, Southern Illinois University Press, 1982, p. 188.

4 For more on this point, see my review of Derrida's *Specters of Marx*, *The European Journal of Philosophy*, vol. 3, no. 3 (December 1995), pp.289–98.

7

Remarks on Deconstruction and Pragmatism[1]

Jacques Derrida

First, I would like to say, even if this shocks certain amongst you and even if I myself took my head in my hands when Richard Rorty said that I was sentimental and that I believed in happiness, I think that he's right. This is something very complicated that I would like to come back to later, but I am very grateful to Richard Rorty for having dared to say something very close to my heart and which is essential to what I am trying to do. Even if it appears very provocative to say it and even if I began by protesting, I think that I was wrong. I am very sentimental and I believe in happiness; and I believe that this has an altogether determinant place in my work. There are so many rich and complex matters to which to respond and I cannot, in improvising, respond to all that has been said. I have the choice between several possibilities and I am going to choose the following: I am going to offer some introductory general remarks after which I will try to respond to some of the questions posed by Simon Critchley, Ernesto Laclau and Richard Rorty.

I will speak French, I am the first to speak French here, and I do this both in order to save time, but also because I think that the question of language is essential to everything that we are discussing here. At bottom, if there are differences between us, this essentially derives from a question of language, not in the sense of different traditions of thinking, national differences, about which there would be a lot to say: for example, my incomprehension with regard to what happens in the United States, whether that concerns Rorty's thinking, or whether that concerns what takes place within American deconstructionism, and whether this derives from an ignorance on my part with regard to their tradition; but it is not this which I am going to insist upon, although it is very important. It is rather the fact that I try to take language seriously, and the contingent fact, of which the consequences are incalculable even if I am not French by birth, that I am bound to the French language and I would like to take account of this in the work of thinking and the work of politics. From this question of language a whole world of consequences follow, at the end of which I will try to come back to our theme.

First of all, the question of argumentation. We are here in order to discuss, and in order to exchange arguments as clear, univocal and communicable as possible. On the other hand, the question that is often raised on the subject of deconstruction is that of argumentation. I am reproached – deconstructionists are reproached – with not arguing or not liking argumentation, etc., etc. This is obviously a defamation. But this defamation derives from the fact that there is argumentation and argumentation, and this is often because in contexts of discussion like the present one where the propositional form, a certain type of propositional form, governs, and where a certain type of micrology is necessarily effaced, where the attention to language is necessarily reduced, argumentation is clearly essential. And what interests me, obviously, are other protocols, other argumentative situations where one does not renounce argumentation simply because one refuses to discuss under certain conditions. As a consequence, I think that the question of argumentation is here central, discussion is here central, and I think that the accusations that are often made against deconstruction derive from the fact that its raising the stakes of argumentation is not taken into account. The fact that it is always a question of reconsidering the protocols and the contexts of argumentation, the questions of competence, the language of discussion, etc.

I think that deconstruction – excuse my frequent usage of this word – shares much, and Simon Critchley noted this very well, with certain motifs of pragmatism. In order to proceed quickly, I recall that from the beginning the question concerning the trace was connected with a certain notion of labour, of doing, and that what I called then *programmatology* tried to link grammatology and pragmatism. And I would say that all the attention given to the performative dimension, which Simon Critchley examined very thoroughly in his essay, is also one of the places of affinity between deconstruction and pragmatism.

Since one of the topics of this volume concerns the distinction between the public and the private and since the questions posed by Simon Critchley were rightly orientated by this question, I would like to say the following, particularly to Richard Rorty to whom I have a great deal of gratitude for the reading, at once tolerant and generous, that he has given of many of my texts. Nevertheless, I must say that I obviously cannot accept the public/private distinction in the way he uses it in relation to my work. This distinction has a long history, of which the genealogy is not so well known, but if I have tried to withdraw a dimension of experience – whether I call it 'singularity', the 'secret' or whatever – from the public or political sphere, and I will come back to this, I would not call this private. In other words, for me the private is not defined by the singular (I do not say personal, because I find this a slightly confused notion) or the secret. In so far as I try to thematize a dimension of the secret that is absolutely irreducible to the public, I also resist the application of the public/private distinction to this dimension.

Let's take the example of literature, since in the 'developmental thesis' of which Simon Critchley spoke and which Rorty now seems clearly to reject, Rorty distinguishes my first works, which are judged to be more philosophical from my later, allegedly more literary works. Rorty returned to this topic when he said that it is necessary to begin by publishing works which reassure the university and that this is also a question of politics and editorial legitimation. This is true, but it is not only that. I believe that my first texts, let's call them more academic or philosophically more reassuring, were also already well beyond the editorial field of social legitimation, and were also a discursive and theoretical (I do not say fundamental or foundational) condition, an irreversibly necessary condition for what came later. It would not only have been impossible to *publish Glas* without *De la grammatologie*, but it would also have been impossible to *write Glas* without the early work. It is here a question of an irreversible philosophical – or quasi-philosophical – trajectory. For me, the texts that are *apparently* more literary, and more tied to the phenomena of natural language, like *Glas* or *La Carte postale*, are not evidence of a retreat towards the private, they are performative problematizations of the public/private distiction. There are a number of examples: in its way, the question of the family in Hegel discussed in *Glas*, of the relation of the family to civil society and the state, can be seen as a performative elaboration of the private on a theoretical, philosophical and political plane; it is not a retreat to private life. *La Carte postale*, the very structure of the text, is one where the distinction between the public and the private is rightly undecidable. And this undecidability poses philosophical problems to philosophy, and political problems, such as what is meant by the public and by the political itself; it poses questions to Heidegger on the concept of destination and the sending of destiny; and when one speaks of destination and the irreducible indeterminateness of destination, we are not simply within literature and within the private, assuming for the moment that one can distinguish the two.

I would like to insist on this because it is a recurrent accusation and, given the constraints of time and context, I will have to speak a little brutally: I have never tried to confuse literature and philosophy or to reduce philosophy to literature. I am very attentive to the difference of space, of history, of historical rites, of logic, of rhetoric, protocols and argumentation. I try to be attentive to this distinction as much as possible. Literature interests me, supposing that, in my own way, I practise it or that I study it in others, precisely as something which is the complete opposite of the expression of private life. Literature is a public institution of recent invention, with a comparatively short history, governed by all sorts of conventions connected to the evolution of law, which allows, in principle, anything to be said. Thus, what defines literature as such, within a certain European history, is profoundly connected with a revolution in law and politics: the principled authorization that anything can be said publicly. In other words, I am not able to separate the invention of literature, the history of literature, from the history of democracy. Under the pretext of fiction, literature must be able to say anything; in other words, it is inseparable from the human rights, from the freedom of expression, etc. One could, if there were time, examine the history of this right that literature has to say anything, and the many limits that are imposed upon it. It is obvious that if democracy remains to come (*à venir*), this right to say anything, even in literature, is not concretely realized or actualized. In any case, literature is the right in principle to say anything, and it is to the great advantage of literature that is an operation at once political, democratic and *philosophical*, to the extent that literature allows one to pose questions that are often repressed in a philosophical context. Naturally, this literary fictionality can, at one and the same moment, make one responsible (I can say anything and thus, not only do I not simply say what I please, but I also pose the question concerning to whom I am responsible), and make one irresponsible (I can say whatever I like and I say it in the guise of a poem, a fiction or a novel). In this responsibility to say anything in literature, there is a political experience as to knowing who is responsible for what and before whom. This is a great good fortune which is linked to the historical adventure of democracy, notably European, and towards which political and philosophical reflection must not be inattentive, and must not confine literature to the private or domestic realm.

I also want to speak of the secret in this regard, because – and at the same time – the right to say anything is said in keeping the secret. For example, in *La Carte postale* anything is said, nobody tells me what to say, but at the same time the secret is kept absolutely. And this secret is not something that I keep within me; it is not me. The secret is not the secret of representation that one keeps in one's head and which one chooses not to tell, it is rather a secret coextensive with the experience of singularity. The secret is irreducible to the public realm – although I do not call it private – and irreducible to publicity and politicization, but at the same time, this secret is that on the basis of which the public realm and the realm of the political can be and remain open. It is on the basis of the secret that I would take up again the question of democracy, because there is a concept of politics and democracy as openness – where all are equal and where the public realm is open to all – which tends to deny, efface or prohibit the secret; in any case, it tends to limit the right to secrecy to the private domain, thereby establishing a culture of privacy (I think that this is the dominant and hegemonic tendency in the history of politics in the West). This is a very serious matter, and it is against this interpretation of democracy that I have attempted to think an experience of the secret and of singularity to which the public realm has no right and no power. Even if we take the example of the most triumphalistic totalitarianism, I believe the secret remains inaccessible and heterogeneous to the public realm. And this heterogeneity is not depoliticizing, it is rather the condition of politicization: it is the way of broaching the question of the political, of the history and genealogy of this concept, with the most concrete consequences.

After these few general remarks, I would now like to turn to some of the themes discussed by Simon Critchley, Ernesto Laclau and Richard Rorty. As Simon Critchley remarked on a couple of occasions, the question of the transcendental has been modified by the 'quasi', and therefore if transcendentality is important to me, it is not simply in its classical sense (although that still interests me greatly). It is because of the highly unstable, and slightly bizarre character of the transcendental that, in *Glas*, I wrote 'quasi-transcendental' and Rodolphe Gasché has made a great deal of this 'quasi'. Now, one of the questions one can pose with regard to this 'quasi' is the connection between it and the question of fiction and literature of which I spoke just now. Do I just speak of this 'quasi' in an ironical, comic or parodic manner, or is it a question of something else? I believe both. There is irony and there is something else. As Simon Critchley said, quoting Rorty, I seem to make noises of both sorts. Now, I claim this right to make noises of both sorts in an absolutely unconditional manner. I absolutely refuse a discourse that would assign me a single code, a single language game, a single context, a single situation; and I claim this right not simply out of caprice or because it is to my taste, but for ethical and political reasons. When I say that quasi-transcendentality is at once ironic and serious, I am being sincere. There is evidently irony in what I do – which I hope is politically justifiable – with regard to academic tradition, the seriousness of the philosophical tradition and the personages of the great philosophers. But, although irony appears to me necessary to what I do, at the same time – and this is a question of memory – I take extremely seriously the issue of philosophical responsibility. I maintain that I am a philosopher and that I want to remain a philosopher, and this philosophical responsibility is something that commands me. Something that I learned from the great figures in the history of philosophy, from Husserl in particular, is the necessity of posing transcendental questions in order not to be held within the fragility of an incompetent empiricist discourse, and thus it is in order to avoid empiricism, positivism and psychologism that it is endlessly necessary to renew transcendental questioning. But such questioning must be renewed in taking account of the possibility of fiction, of accidentality and contingency, thereby ensuring that this new form of transcendental questioning only mimics the phantom of classical transcendental seriousness without renouncing that which, within this phantom, constitutes an essential heritage. And I believe that what I said earlier about fiction and literature is indispensable for the elaboration of this quasi-transcendentality. This is notably the case when I think of how I have been regularly lead back over the past thirty years, and in relation to quite different problems, to the necessity of defining the transcendental condition of possibility as also being a condition of impossibility. This is something that I am not able to annul. Clearly, to define a function of possibility as a function of impossibility, that is, to define a possibility as its impossibility, is highly unorthodox from a traditional transcendental perspective, and yet this is what reappears all the time, when I come back to the question of the fatality of aporia. I think I am in complete agreement with what Ernesto said about the question of transcendentality from a political point of view.

A word on the important theme of emancipation. Simon Critchley claimed that I said something surprising when I remarked, in 'Force of Law', that I refuse to renounce the great classical discourse of emancipation. I believe that there is an enormous amount to do today for emancipation, in all domains and all the areas of the world and society. Even if I would not wish to inscribe the discourse of emancipation into a teleology, a metaphysics, an eschatology, or even a classical messianism, I none the less believe that there is no ethico-political decision or gesture without what I would call a 'Yes' to emancipation, to the discourse of emancipation, and even, I would add, to some messianicity. It is necessary here to explain a little what I mean by messianicity.

It is not a question of a messianism that one could easily translate in Judaeo-Christian or Islamic terms, but rather of a messianic structure that belongs to all language. There is no language without the performative dimension of the promise, the minute I open my mouth I am in the promise. Even if I say that 'I don't believe in truth' or whatever, the minute I open my mouth there is a 'believe me' at work. Even when I lie, and perhaps especially when I lie, there is a 'believe me' in play. And this 'I promise you that I am speaking the truth' is a messianic apriori, a promise which, even if it is not kept, even if one knows that it cannot be kept, takes place and *qua* promise is messianic. And from this point of view, I do not see how one can pose the question of ethics if one renounces the motifs of emancipation and the messianic. Emancipation is once again a vast question today and I must say that I have no tolerance for those who – deconstructionist or not – are ironical with regard to the grand discourse of emancipation. This attitude has always distressed and irritated me. I do not want to renounce this discourse.

Picking up on a word used on several occasions by Simon Critchley and Richard Rorty, I would not call this attitude utopian. The messianic experience of which I spoke takes place here and now; that is, the fact of promising and speaking is an event that takes place here and now and is not utopian. This happens in the singular event of engagement, and when I speak of democracy to come (*la démocratie à venir*) this does not mean that tomorrow democracy will be realized, and it does not refer to a future democracy, rather it means that there is an engagement with regard to democracy which consists in recognizing the irreducibility of the promise when, in the messianic moment, 'it can come' ('*ça peut venir*'). There is the future (*il y a de l'avenir*). There is something to come (*il y a à venir*). That can happen ... that can happen, and I promise in opening the future or in leaving the future open. This is not utopian, it is what takes place here and now, in a here and now that I regularly try to dissociate from the present. Although this is difficult to explain briefly in this context, I try to dissociate the theme of singularity happening here and now from the theme of presence and, for me, there can be a here and now without presence.

I am completely in agreement with everything that Ernesto Laclau has said on the question of hegemony and power, and I also agree that in the most reassuring and disarming discussion and persuasion, force and violence are present. None the less, I think that there is, in the opening of a context of argumentation and discussion, a reference – unknown, indeterminate, but none the less thinkable – to disarmament. I agree that such disarmament is never simply present, even in the most pacific moment of persuasion, and therefore that a certain force and violence is irreducible, but none the less this violence can only be practised and can only appear as such on the basis of a non-violence, a vulnerability, an exposition. I do not believe in non-violence as a descriptive and determinable experience, but rather as an irreducible promise and of the relation to the other as essentially non-instrumental. This is not the dream of a beatifically pacific relation, but of a certain experience of friendship perhaps unthinkable today and unthought within the historical determination of friendship in the West. This is a friendship, what I sometimes call an *aimance*, that excludes violence; a non-appropriative relation to the other that occurs without violence and on the basis of which all violence detaches itself and is determined.

Thus, and this is the point that I wanted to emphasize in relation to Ernesto Laclau, once it is granted that violence is *in fact* irreducible, it becomes necessary – and this is the moment of politics – to have rules, conventions and stabilizations of power. All that a deconstructive point of view tries to show, is that since convention, institutions and consensus are stabilizations (sometimes stabilizations of great duration, sometimes micro-stabilizations), this means that they are stabilizations of something essentially unstable and chaotic. Thus, it becomes necessary to stabilize precisely because stability is not natural; it is because there is instability that stabilization becomes necessary; it is because there is chaos that there is a need for stability. Now, this chaos and instability, which is fundamental, founding and irreducible, is at once naturally the worst against which we struggle with laws, rules, conventions, politics and provisional hegemony, but at the same time it is a chance, a chance to change, to destabilize. If there were continual stability, there would be no need for politics, and it is to the extent that stability is not natural, essential or substantial, that politics exists and ethics is possible. Chaos is at once a risk and a chance, and it is here that the possible and the impossible cross each other.

I would like to come back to what Ernesto Laclau said about the subject and the decision. The question here is whether it is through the decision that one becomes a subject who decides something. At the risk of appearing provocative, I would say that once one poses the question in that form and one imagines that the who and the what of the subject can be determined in advance, then there is no decision. In other words, the decision, if there is such a thing, must neutralize if not render impossible in advance the who and the what. If one knows, and if it is a subject that knows who and what, then the decision is simply the application of a law. In other words, if there is a decision, it presupposes that the subject of the decision does not yet exist and neither does the object. Thus with regard to the subject and the object, there will never be a decision. I think this summarizes a little what Ernesto Laclau proposed when he said that the decision presupposes identification, that is to say that the subject does not exist prior to the decision but when I decide I invent the subject. Every time I decide, if a decision is possible, I invent the who, and I decide who decides what; at this moment the question is not the who or the what but rather that of the decision, if there is such a thing. Thus I agree that identification is indispensable, but this is also a process of disidentification, because if the decision is identification then the decision also destroys itself.

As a consequence, one must say that in the relationship to the other, who is indeed the one in the name of which and of whom the decision is taken, the other remains inappropriable to the process of identification. This is why I would say that the transcendental subject is that which renders the decision impossible. The decision is barred when there is something like a transcendental subject. In order to take things a bit further I would say that if duty is conceived of as a simple relation between the categorical imperative and a determinable subject, then duty is evaded. If I act in accordance with duty in the Kantian sense, I do not act and furthermore I do not act in accordance with duty. It is easy to see that this raises many paradoxes and many aporias. That is to say that the decision, if there is such a thing, cannot be taken in the name of some *thing*. For example, if one says that the decision is taken in the name of the other, that does not mean that the other is going to take on my responsibility when I say that I always decide in the name of the other. To take a decision in the name of the other in no way at all lightens my responsibility, on the contrary, and Levinas is very forceful on this point, my responsibility is *accused* by the fact that it is the other in the name of which I decide. This is an alienation much more radical than the classical meaning given to this term. I decide in the name of the other without this in the least lightening my responsibility; on the contrary the other is the origin of my responsibility without it being determinable in terms of an identity. The decision announces itself from the perspective of a much more radical alterity.

I would now like to try very rapidly to respond directly to points made by Richard Rorty on the use of the word deconstruction. On the one hand, I have often said I do not need to use this word and I often wondered why it should have interested so many people. However, as time passes, and when I see so many people trying to get rid of this word, I ask myself whether there is not perhaps something in it. I would ask you how you would explain why this word, which, for essential reasons, and I agree with Rorty, is meaningless and without reference, could impose itself? How is it that something 'x', which does not have a stable meaning or reference, becomes indispensable in a certain finite, but open, context, during a certain period of time, for a certain number of actors?

When you said that you do not see the necessary relation between deconstruction and pragmatism, I would say 'yes and no'. I have the same feeling as Rorty in the sense that deconstruction, in the manner in which it is utilized and put to work, is always a highly unstable and almost empty motif. And I would insist that everyone can use this motif as they please to serve quite different political perspectives, which would seem to mean that deconstruction is politically neutral. But, the fact that deconstruction is apparently politically neutral allows, on the one hand, a reflection on the nature of the political, and on the other hand, and this is what interests me in deconstruction, a hyper-politicization. Deconstruction is hyper-politicizing in following paths and codes which are clearly not traditional, and I believe it awakens politicization in the way I mentioned above, that is, it permits us to think the political and think the democratic by granting us the space necessary in order not to be enclosed in the latter. In order to continue to pose the question of the political, it is necessary to withdraw something from the political and the same thing for democracy, which, of course, makes democracy a very paradoxical concept.

To move on to a question that Rorty raised in discussion concerning the weakening of the political left in the United States, this would demand a great deal of analysis and perhaps Rorty is right in seeing such a weakening. But even if Rorty is right, my hope, as a man of the left, is that certain elements of deconstruction will have served or – because the struggle continues, particularly in the United States – *will* serve to politicize or repoliticize the left with regard to positions which are not simply academic. I hope – and if I can continue to contribute a little to this I will be very content – that the political left in universities in the United States, France and elsewhere, will gain politically by employing deconstruction. To a certain extent, and in an unequal way, this is a movement that is already under way.

I do not believe that the themes of undecidability or infinite responsibility are romantic, as Rorty claimed. Of course, I can see how one might associate these motifs with a certain dramatic romantic pathos, but personally I would prefer this not to be the case. The necessity for thinking to traverse interminably the experience of undecidability can, I think, be quite coolly demonstrated in an analysis of the ethical or political decision. If we analysed the concepts of decision and responsibility in a cool manner, we would find that undecidability is irreducible within them. If one does not take rigorous account of undecidability, it will not only be the case that one cannot act, decide or assume responsibility, but one will not even be able to *think* the concepts of decision and responsibility. To come back to the question of the decision, this is a subject for argumentation and I would like to be very argumentative on the question of the decision. The same thing is true of responsibility, whether that is a question of Levinas or of what I owe to him. I believe that we cannot give up on the concept of infinite responsibility, as Rorty seemed to do at the end of his essay, when he wrote of Levinas as a blind spot in my work. I would say, for Levinas and for myself, that if you give up the infinitude of responsibility, there is no responsibility. It is because we act and we live in infinitude that the responsibility with regard to the other (*autrui*) is irreducible. If responsibility were not infinite, if every time that I have to take an ethical or political decision with regard to the other (*autrui*) this were not infinite, then I would not be able to engage myself in an infinite debt with regard to each singularity. I owe myself infinitely to each and every singularity. If responsibility were not infinite, you could not have moral and political problems. There are only moral and political problems, and everything that follows from this, from the moment when responsibility is not limitable. As a consequence, whatever choice I might make, I cannot say with good conscience that I have made a good choice or that I have assumed my responsibilities. Every time that I hear someone say that 'I have taken a decision', or 'I have assumed my responsibilities', I am suspicious because if there is responsibility or decision one cannot determine them as such or have certainty or good conscience with regard to them. If I conduct myself particularly well with regard to someone, I know that it is to the detriment of an other; of one nation to the detriment of another nation, of one family to the detriment of another family, of my friends to the detriment of other friends or non-friends, etc. This is the infinitude that inscribes itself within responsibility; otherwise there would be no ethical problems or decisions. And this is why undecidability is not a moment to be traversed and overcome. Conflicts of duty – and there is only duty in conflict – are interminable and even when I take my decision and do something, undecidability is not at an end. I know that I have not done enough and it is in this way that morality continues, that history and politics continue. There is politicization or ethicization because undecidability is not simply a moment to be overcome by the occurrence of the decision. Undecidability continues to inhabit the decision and the latter does not close itself off from the former. The relation to the other does not close itself off, and it is because of this that there is history and one tries to act politically.

When Rorty says, for example, that he does not think that change is dramatic and that things just are the way they are, I can understand what he says. Indeed, in the conduct of our private lives and in relation to the great events of history and politics, our usual response is to say, *c'est comme celà*, that's the way things are. One has the impression that choices and decisions are of no importance and we could provide a thousand examples of this. But, the fact that this is the way things are does not mean that choice is simply an epiphenomenon or that it does not engage infinite responsibility. I believe that we should try to think 'the way things are' together with infinite responsibility, impossible choices and madness. I do not think that we can choose between the two alternatives, and we cannot conclude that there is no choice from the fact that this is 'the way things are'. Does Rorty renounce the question of choice? Would he say, in the final account, that there is no choice and that although choice is a word that is employed, that is also just 'the way things are'? I often use the expression *s'il y en a*, when I speak of our relation to choice, decision and responsibility, but this does not mean that these things do not exist or that they are impossible, it means rather that our relation to matters like choice, decision and responsibility is not a theoretical, constative or determinate relation. It is always a suspended relation. Even when I believe myself to have opted for a decision, I do not know if I have in fact taken a decision, but it is necessary that I refer myself to the possibility of this decision and think it, *s'il y en a*. I would say the same thing about responsibility and this is linked to what I said above about the 'quasi'. We have a relation to things as they are for which a determinate or constative truth, a constative presence, is impossible, and at the same time we are not able to renounce these things, we should not renounce them.

I say this in order to underline the fact that I would not be in agreement when Rorty speaks of philosophy as depoliticizing. I would also, very quickly and as a final word, come back to what Rorty said about 'The Politics of Friendship' and clarify that when I speak of virile homosexuality as a dominant concept in discussions of friendship and politics, what interests me is the fact that the historically transmitted concepts of love and friendship are essentially heterosexual, but that there can be no friendship amongst women and that there is only friendship amongst men. This is the phallogocentric concept of friendship that has dominated the tradition, and defines it as homosexual and virile and which always connects political responsibility to young men. It is this that has dominated the concept of friendship and it is this that I wanted to place in question.

Note

1 Translated by Simon Critchley. This text was originally presented in French and the translation has not sought to erase traces of its oral delivery.